The Last Voyage of the Lusitania

The Last Voyage of the Lusitania

A. A. Hoehling and Mary Hoehling

BONANZA BOOKS
New York

This 1991 edition is published by Bonanza Books,
distributed by Outlet Book Company, Inc., a Random House
Company, 225 Park Avenue South, New York, New York 10003,
by arrangement with the authors.

Printed and bound in the United States of America

Library of Congress Cataloging-in-Publication Data

Hoehling, A. A. (Adolph A.)
    The last voyage of the Lusitania / A.A. Hoehling and Mary
Hoehling.
    p. cm.
  Reprint. Originally published: New York: Holt, c1956
  Includes bibliographical references and index.
  ISBN 0-517-05786-7
  1. Lusitania (Steamship)   I. Hoehling, Mary Duprey, 1914-
II. Title.
D592.L8H6 1991
940.4'514—dc20   90-25109
                                                        CIP

8   7   6   5   4   3   2   1

To the Memory of
the Lost Members of the Gun Crew of
the SS *James Harrod*
in World War II

The dead have not lived and died in vain. They have brought us all a little nearer together— we think better of our kind . . .

—*Elbert Hubbard*

PROLOGUE

～～～～～～～～～～～～～～～～～～～

On May 8, 1915, Americans awoke to find an era abruptly ended. Something had happened which would affect their immediate future and the destiny of the world.

The afternoon before, the huge Cunarder *Lusitania* had been torpedoed by a German submarine off the Irish coast. More than half of those aboard perished, including Americans, children, and a number of people whose names were known to almost everyone.

The *Lusitania* became more than one of the world's great disasters. It was a Concord Bridge of 1915, a rallying cry like the "Alamo" and the *"Maine."* Within two years, resigned to the fact that its comfortable, insular years could never be brought back, the United States was projected into the European war and an entirely new position of world leadership.

Perhaps no other ship before or after the *Lusitania* so profoundly altered nautical history. In the annals of marine engineering she occupies a niche alongside of Fulton's *Clermont.* With her revolutionary steam turbines she pushed transatlantic speeds up several knots. Marine architects everywhere hurried to their drafting boards, for the *Lusitania* had rewritten the books.

Superliners today like the *United States* and the *Queen Elizabeth* have the same kind of turbine engines that *Lusitania* pioneered. They also may thank her for elevators, cabin telephones, complete electrification, and even an ancestral kind of air-conditioning—modern refinements few American hotels could advertise then.

Except for passing references in history books, the story of the *Lusitania* is strangely forgotten. Scholars must dig into musty files for the yellowing, hysterical pamphlets and articles which tell fragments of the incredible tragedy. Yet in 1915 the name of the huge ship was on everyone's lips. It aroused Main Street to adulthood and sent it forth into the world.

. . . This, then, is the documentary story of the fateful voyage of a ship that helped to change a century.

CHAPTER 1

An Irish spring morning, misty and mild, dawned May 7, 1915. From Waterford, at St. George's Channel into the Irish Sea, all the way to lonely Fastnet Rock, at Ireland's southwest tip, the fog draped its light gray shroud over the flat waters.

Along Ireland's south coast, most fishing boats were warped to their docks. Sea gulls, with broad, black-tipped wings, squawked as they swooped out of the fog to dive for herring. It was like almost any day on the sea—salty, dank, immense, and timeless.

Yet, for a young U-boat skipper, blond and round-faced as a schoolboy, it wasn't just *any* day. Kapitanleutnant Walther Schwieger's *U-20*, one week out of Emden, was surfaced fifteen miles south of a prominent peninsula, the Old Head of Kinsale.

Schwieger had found good hunting in these fishing grounds, only twenty-five miles west of Queenstown. In the past forty-eight hours he had torpedoed and sunk two Harrison Line steamers and shelled a sailing ship.

It was his first patrol aboard a U-boat in a war not yet a

year old. His *U-20* had relieved the *U-24* and the *U-32*. They were now somewhere in the coastal waters of the British Isles, beating toward the North Sea and home.

Other German submarines were on station in a death struggle to sever Britain's lifelines of commerce. The *U-27* had sailed with the *U-20*. The *U-23* had bagged four vessels a few days before off the same Irish coasts. And Kapitanleutnant Hersing—who had sunk three British fighting ships in the opening months of the war to become Germany's first submarine hero—was en route in *U-21* through these waters to the Adriatic.

The *U-39* was also on the prowl. She had sunk, among other vessels, the Wilson Liner *Truro* off Day Island, Scotland. The English crew, in their lifeboats, saw the U-boat's number on the conning tower before she submerged. Undoubtedly there were still others enforcing the blockade, and responsible for urgent British Admiralty warnings which had been flashed repeatedly across the airwaves for the past twelve hours.

They all gave many indications that they were waiting for something special this morning in May.

Sparking the first rounds in Admiral von Tirpitz's warfare on merchant shipping, the U-boat crews were at the peak of morale. The thirty-five men and three other officers aboard Schwieger's 650-ton *Unterseeboot* thought of their "little nutshell" as a happy boat, even a "kindly boat."

They slept by the torpedoes, some with pet dogs at their feet. They lovingly gave to the cylindrical messengers of sudden doom such names as "Bertha," "Shining Emma," and "Yellow Mary." Each torpedo carried 290 pounds of a terrible new explosive called trotyl, and had a range of nearly four miles.

Now the *U-20* was on the surface, charging its tiers of wet-cell storage batteries, renewing oxygen below decks, driving out the persistent mixture of cooking, machine oil, carbonic gas, and human-breath smells. A U-boat was more than a confined world of a thousand mysterious wheels, gauges, and gadgets; it was as well a chamber of odors.

Kapitanleutnant Schwieger, his leather jacket unbuttoned, stood in the conning tower and enjoyed the soft morning air. There was a look of disarming mildness on his open face.

The diesels hummed reassuringly as the U-boat rolled cradle-like in the surface swells. The sea bed, sandy and swirling with offshoots from the Gulf Stream, was only 300 feet below.

About noon the fog thinned, then cleared off. Now, through his binoculars, Schwieger could discern details of the Old Head of Kinsale. It rose 256 feet out of the water and jutted three miles seaward from the mainland, just west of the Bandon River.

It was a perfect landmark on which to take a sure bearing, as was Seven Heads Point scarcely ten miles west. Schwieger could make out dim shapes of houses on Kinsale, and fishing shacks along the shores. The bright spring sun silhouetted details of the Irish coast like an engraving.

With clearing weather, the U-boat had lost its anonymity. It was naked to any warship that might steam over the horizon, as indeed one had earlier. Schwieger kept a sharp lookout through his binoculars around the full 360 degrees of the compass. As the sun burned warmer and warmer, he removed his jacket. The gulls swooped low to inspect this mechanical fish, called and wheeled again.

The sea smelled good. Schwieger had to like it; for an indefinite future it was to be his home. In the conning tower he munched a luncheon of sausage and potato soup. From below came the tinny gramophone strains of the popular "Rose of Stamboul." It managed, as only a German rendition could, to blend rollicking ballad with Wagnerian overtures.

Life seemed serene and altogether pleasant.

Then, shortly before 2:00 P.M. by his watch, Schwieger picked up something in his binoculars—a rapidly materializing speck hauling in from the west. He decided first it was the masts and funnels of two destroyers. He took a second look and wrote in his log:

> Right ahead appear four funnels and two masts of a steamer with course vertical to us. [She steered from SSW coming toward Galley Head.] Ship is made out to be a large passenger steamer.

The U-boat came alive as the tingling order "Diving Stations" electrified its crew. Those in the conning tower scurried almost as one man down the steel ladder to the control room below.

The *U-20* could make only nine knots submerged, compared with a relatively fast fifteen on the surface. Yet below the water's surface was where she belonged. She was safer down there. Even as the heavy steel door clanged, sealing off the conning tower, Schwieger received the engineer's report by voice tube:

"Hands at diving stations! All clear for diving!"

"Flood!" Schwieger snapped.

Petty officers at a station beneath the control room spun hand wheels to open the vents. At the same time pumps forced air out of ballast tanks.

"Both motors slow ahead!" Schwieger ordered. Now the electric motors were geared in from the diesels, which could operate only on the surface, where carbon-monoxide exhaust could be dissipated into open air.

"Tanks exhausted of air and filling with water!" the engineer next reported.

Under an inrush of tons of sea water the *U-20* was assuming a sloping angle, familiar to the veterans of her crew, as she slid, creaking, under the surface swells.

Schwieger watched through his periscope the familiar spectacle of waves rising and breaking over the glass above. The water rushed at him in dark gray rivulets, then foamed bright again as he leveled off at approximately thirty-three feet, periscope depth.

"Rudder amidships! Steady as you go! Full speed ahead!"

A growing throb of power was felt as the electric motors spun their armatures faster. The submarine shook as it shot through the waters.

Again he noted:

2:05 P.M. Submerged to 11 meters and travelled with high speed on course converging toward steamer, hoping she would change course to starboard along Irish coast.

Schwieger was racing to get in position so he could effectively fire a bow torpedo.

"Up . . . up. . . . Stop. . . . Down. . . . Up. . . . Stop. . . . Down. . . . Stop . . . down . . . carry on . . . !"

His orders rang out in an unceasing monotone, as he adjusted the trim of his submarine with the precision of a surgeon.

He looked away from the eyepiece of the periscope for fractions of a second to study the depth-gauge manometer beside it. Once or twice he tapped it to make sure.

The gramophone was shut off now. The crew was tense,

serious. With the hatch battened tight and sealed by a water-proof gasket, the *U-20* was already assuming its familiar rank odor. Lurking somewhere in the background was the added taint of a strong cigar.

Her quarry was looming larger and larger, almost filling the optical glass screen of the periscope. Still, Walther Schwieger noted, he did not know "who" the giant ship was.

But if the U-boat Kapitanleutnant did not know the identity of the 32,000-ton liner, he at least had the advantage over Captain William Thomas Turner. For neither that veteran Cunard captain, a seadog's seadog, nor anyone else on board the *Lusitania* knew even that they were being watched.

As Schwieger stalked his 790-foot-long target, Captain Turner decided to take a four-point bearing on the Old Head of Kinsale, now looming hazily off the port bow. It was a positive way of checking position, requiring the better part of an hour.

Captain Turner gave orders for a new, steady course, slightly altering the existing one to 87 degrees or almost due east. At the same time he maintained a speed of exactly eighteen knots, considerably lower than the *Lusitania's* top speed of twenty-five plus, which had once made her the queen of the Atlantic. On board her it was about 2:00 P.M., Greenwich Mean Time.

Schwieger, whose watch was set one hour later, wrote:

> 2:50 P.M. The steamer turns starboard, directs her course toward Queenstown, and makes possible an approach for a shot. Ran at high speed until 3:00 P.M. in order to gain position directly ahead.

Turner had unwittingly complied with Schwieger's wish. The target presented was a U-boat captain's dream: moving in an undeviating line, at a moderate fixed speed, it looked like a blackboard diagram in naval navigation school.

While the liner and the submarine were in this way converging, most of the 1257 passengers were either finishing lunch or taking a turn around the vessel's avenues of decking. Some were watching the light green of the Irish coastline, so close now that houses were clearly visible. Others were packing, for they were due at Liverpool by breakfast.

Together with her crew, there were almost 2000 souls aboard, but still 1000 less than capacity. The passenger list especially underscored the diversity of human beings which an ocean liner brings together. Yet they had one thing in common: everyone had some pressing reason to travel to a belligerent nation through a declared war zone.

There was aboard, for example, one of the richest men in the world, who had a date in London with some horses. There was a Chicago manufacturer bent on developing foreign markets for beer machinery, against the threat of Prohibition in America. There was an eccentric but famous writer-philosopher from upstate New York; a celebrated producer who had made the theater big business; an Arctic explorer; a woman spiritualist hastening to a meeting of the Psychical Society in London; a manufacturer of automobiles and a man who sold chains for them; a mother and father and their six children; and hundreds of little people, and little children, of whom the world had never heard before.

From the control room Schwieger watched the ship constantly. Gentlemanly and kind as he might have been under different circumstances, his obligation now was to destroy the mammoth vessel. Sentiment, or even reflective thought, had no place in the impersonal articles of war of his country nor of his enemies.

Now Schwieger maneuvered into final position. He would have to fire a torpedo or forfeit his opportunity. The metallic report crackled through the voice tube from the torpedo officer:

"The torpedoes are cleared for firing!"

The reply from the captain:

"We are at them!"

He was dead on target. The huge liner, with smoke wisping from her stack as she cleaved the waters into two bow waves, dominated the periscope. The white of her superstructure shone like a beacon.

Schwieger wondered how he could miss!

CHAPTER 2

Friday, the last day of April, 1915, Charles A. Plamondon and his wife Mary had stepped off the train in New York's Pennsylvania Station. He was a stocky, mustached Midwesterner of fifty-eight, and a busy man. He had several dates, among them a most important one for the next day: to sail on the *Lusitania*.

"Morning, Am," he said to his son. Young Ambrose, a senior at Columbia University Law School, had come directly from his room in Furnald Hall.

"How's the baby?" Am asked.

His father, president of the A. Plamondon Company, machinery manufacturers in Chicago, had been delayed two weeks awaiting the arrival of a new granddaughter, just christened Blanche. Already he had missed two sailings. For him it meant putting off an evil day, since he disliked ocean voyaging. He claimed to be the world's worst sailor, and only pressing business would draw him from his beloved lake-front home on the near North Side of Chicago.

With Prohibition approaching, Plamondon had been forced to seek the European market for his brewery machinery. To discuss this matter he was to meet in Liverpool with agents of Dublin's Guinness Stout Company. Plamondon had asked his wife to accompany him, for he intended this trip to be a vacation as well.

The trio walked through the dusty morning sunlight which shafted onto the cement concourse. It was warmer here than beside Lake Michigan, and the manufacturer pushed his dark bowler hat back on his head. He inquired how the war was going, and Am told him that the British had beaten off new attacks on Hill 60, that around Ypres the fighting was bloody.

Plamondon breakfasted with his wife and son at the Waldorf-Astoria in their seventh-floor suite. It wasn't entirely pleasant, for the younger Plamondon reminded his father of his desire to join the French Foreign Legion. Ambrose referred, as one motivation, to the daily samplings of war horror stories that were issuing from London—the Germans "crucifying" Canadian soldiers, raping Belgian women and shooting their husbands in cold blood. . . .

"What information do you expect to come out of London?" his father sniffed. "They're English there—and at war with Germany."

By taking out his pocket diary to make last-minute entries, he indicated he was done with the conversation. Then he added:

"Why don't you take a trip to San Francisco and see the Exposition? Anyhow, wait till we return—we'll only be a few weeks."

Time was moving. Even as sailors and engineers were readying many ships for sea along New York's waterfronts, the people who were to sail on them also had much to do.

Mrs. Plamondon was going to Lane Bryant's, then to the white sale at Wanamaker's. She enjoyed just walking down Fifth Avenue to see what other women were wearing.

Am himself walked into a mild, cloudy morning, back to classes. As he looked down the endless chain of four- and five-storied brownstone and brick houses along Park Avenue, he decided to thwart his father and enlist anyway.

He hurried across Madison, then Fifth Avenue, ducking in front of carriages, high-top cabs, and double-decker buses, toward the Seventh Avenue subway which would carry him to Morningside Heights. The air smelled nostalgically of spring and horses, of warming pavements, asphalt, gasoline, and even the musty odor that old buildings themselves exude.

At about the same time a lady in Taftville, Connecticut, was preparing to leave on a journey of her own. Elizabeth Duckworth had packed two huge straw suitcases so full that Bill Smith, her son-in-law, feared they would burst. En route to New York to sail for England in the morning, she would spend the night with friends in Brooklyn.

Bill was hard put to keep up with the stride of this firm-jawed, stalwart woman as she swung past the textile mill where he worked. She had served there, too, as a cotton weaver until recently. They continued down Norwich Avenue to the electric trolley which would take her to New London and the train.

There were no tears in Elizabeth's blue eyes as she relieved Bill of the one bulging case he had managed. In a twinkling the trolley picked her up and carried her out of sight, round the curve and down the hill of the small mill town.

As the car rattled past the greenery, through the tiny

towns along the Connecticut River, and across rippling brooks, Elizabeth's thoughts returned to Blackburn, England, where she was born fifty-two years before. Big, smoky, centuries-stained Blackburn, in Lancashire, was one of the cotton-weaving centers of the world.

". . . I can see the mums in the window inside my mother's house, and the evening light slanting over the kitchen range after work when she brewed us a pot of tea . . . I remember the soft coal smoke and fog that drifted in from the Irish Sea, the hard-working people, and the dark houses where they huddled around grates in winter, the smudged-faced children in ragged clothes, the food lines when times were bad at the mills. . . ."

Elizabeth Duckworth was going back because she was homesick. She didn't care if her son-in-law had told her it was too dangerous to sail across. She always had been independent, and at fifty-two it was too late to change. It wasn't easy to lose a husband . . . and then another one.

By the time the trolley arrived in New London, she was warm, and she wished she had worn a lighter cotton—not this dark solid-color with the tight collar. She removed her close-brimmed straw hat and held it in her lap.

At the station in New London she looked once more at her precious passage—a steerage ticket on the *Lusitania*—and put it back in her tightly clutched purse. Then at the New York, New Haven, and Hartford window, she paid for her one-way fare to New York—$3.04.

In a few minutes the steam locomotive was ringing its bell. It pounded around the curve along New London's waterfront and came to a halt at the platform. Elizabeth hoisted her ponderous baggage onto the train.

Once in the dusty plush coach seat she leaned back, unbuttoned her collar, and reached in her purse for the ham sandwich Bill had prepared. Then she smiled. She could almost smell the factory smoke of Blackburn.

While Elizabeth Duckworth was eating, a family trio sat down to lunch in the oppressive Victorian atmosphere of the Gotham Hotel in New York. The group consisted of Mr. and Mrs. Allen D. Loney and their fourteen-year-old daughter Virginia Bruce.

Loney was an American who had taken up residence in England. Though a well-known member of the hunting set, it was some time since he had ridden to hounds across the fields beyond Northampton's spires. He was driving now for the Red Cross in France.

Mrs. Loney, also an American, had returned to the States because she was homesick. When she became more homesick for Allen, he came to New York to bring her and his daughter back to Northampton.

He was pleased on many counts. In addition to being reunited with his family, he would have a sea voyage, a vacation, and brief respite from the dangers of driving close to the front, where stray shells might blast one into eternity at any moment. Virginia Bruce was more than pleased at the prospect of a trip on the big, fast *Lusitania*—London in a week!

Downtown, at the foot of 11th Street, in the rank heart of the meat-packing district, alongside cement-fronted Pier 54, the 702 men and women who comprised the crew were trying to ready the *Lusitania* for her voyage so that she could indeed push her long, graceful prow up the Mersey River in a week's time.

As chief engineer, the walrus-mustached, veteran Archibald Bryce made his rounds far below in a world of heavy grease and shiny metal. He noted in the log—once more— that six of the vessel's twenty-five boilers were cold, and would remain that way. There were hardly enough stokers to fire the nineteen mammoth boilers which were hot. This crossing would necessarily be far slower than the record run of four-and-one-half days in 1909.

Coal barges alongside the ship were bunkering her with 1000 tons less than her great 7000-ton coal capacity, a capacity that in itself was considerably heavier than the entire gross weight of the average freighter. All considered, it meant a reduction in log speed to about twenty-one knots. Yet everyone agreed with Captain Turner that the *Lusitania,* fettered as she was, still held a six-knot margin over the fastest U-boat.

On the afternoon of April 30, 1915, that seemed margin enough.

The economy was necessary, Alfred A. Booth, Cunard's youthful Chairman of the Board, explained, since wartime travel was lean. Steerage, or Third, was only one-third booked, spelling a loss to the company if the voyage were to be made at top speed with a full crew.

The *Lusitania* was nearly ready for sea. In the late-Georgian First Class lounge, a new coat of polish had been applied to the inlaid mahogany. The heavy velvet drapes were freshly cleaned.

From the balconied dome of the Louis VI First Class dining saloon, nine painted muses smiled down. Like the visitors who were touring the ship, they seemed pleased with the sumptuous saloon.

Whatever noises the crew caused in their 'tween-decks ministrations provided but a contrast to the clamor of the stevedores as they filled the holds.

An assorted cargo was going on board, making the *Lusitania* in this respect vaguely kin to the most cosmopolitan tramp steamer. In her manifest were such items as 200,000 pounds of sheet brass, 111,762 pounds of copper, odd lots of different kinds of machinery from Boston, 217,157 pounds of cheese, 342,165 pounds of beef, 43,614 pounds of lard, 185,040 pounds of bacon, 205 barrels of Connecticut oysters, 25 barrels of lubricating oil, 655 packages of confectionery, several bales of leather sides, 5 packages of automobiles and automobile parts, and 17 packages of dental goods. An additional hodge-podge included crates of chickens, to be eaten during the voyage. Much of the cargo, like the machinery, brass, leather sides, and oysters, had come down from New England.

Also being hoisted aboard was another type of cargo that some persons—the Germans for example—might have classified as war contraband. This consisted of 4200 cases of small-caliber rifle ammunition and somewhat more than 100 cases of empty shrapnel shells and unloaded fuses. They had all been listed with the Collector of the Port of New York, Dudley Field Malone, as was the rest of the cargo.

Altogether, the *Lusitania*'s cargo was valued at a relatively modest 750,000 dollars. Rumors had it that more than 6,000,-000 dollars in gold bullion was locked in a strong room in a lower deck; but it was not on the manifest.

As the afternoon waned, the cargo still arrived in deep,

greasy nets, while seamen continued to dab white paint onto the liner's already-glistening superstructure.

In another part of New York the Allied cause was being served by a pretty Belgian woman. Marie de Page was addressing a meeting of the Special Relief Society at the home of Mrs. Charles B. Alexander, 4 West 58th Street. The wife of Dr. Antoine de Page of Brussels, Mme de Page was concluding a successful nation-wide tour on behalf of Belgian relief and the Belgian hospital at La Panne. The latter, known as the "Queen's Hospital," was directed by her husband and was already filled with wounded soldiers.

Pledges now totaled well over 100,000 dollars in cash and half that again in supplies. Mme de Page had considered her reception in Pittsburgh a few days ago "overwhelming," as she had those in Washington and many other American cities during two busy months.

This afternoon, as May breezes from Central Park wafted through the opened, lace-curtained windows and the traffic of Fifth Avenue chugged and clopped past, Mme de Page gave a final description of impoverished, wartorn Belgium. She could speak of the war with conviction, for one of her sons, Lucien, was fighting on the Western Front.

The room was quiet when she finally thanked her audience and told them she must hurry to her hotel to pack. "I am sailing for home tomorrow on the *Lusitania*," she said. Hers had been a last-minute reservation. In order to complete her business in America, she had canceled passage on the *Lapland*, which had sailed the day before.

At the same hour Alfred Gwynne Vanderbilt, whom some thought worth nearly 100,000,000 dollars, was dressing for dinner in the Vanderbilt Hotel on lower Park Avenue. His valet, Ronald Denyer, had just packed his master's luggage for a three weeks' trip to London.

Elsewhere in the suite, nursemaids were tucking Alfred, Jr., and George Vanderbilt into bed. Goings and comings were so commonplace in their father's life that he would make no more of bidding them good-by than if he were merely going to his Oakland Farm stables in Newport.

Nevertheless, he was a good and kindly father to Alfred and George and also to Billy, who now lived with his first wife. Vanderbilt provided them all with a magic nurseryland of toys, and friends witnessed the enjoyment he obtained from playing with them in his infrequent leisure moments.

This time his London stables were taking him from home and his second wife, the former Mrs. Margaret Emerson McKim. There always seemed matters to be tended to where horses were concerned. As a director of the International Horse Show Association, he was due to meet with other directors in London. Officers of the National Horse Show Association, with whom he had conferred this afternoon, had agreed that the war was going well enough to resume the fall show, canceled the year before.

Handsome, thirty-eight-year-old Vanderbilt contemplated his visits to England with mixed feelings. The suicide there six years ago of a St. Louis beauty underscored a situation which already had left a bad taste in Court of St. James circles. The woman, wife of a consul, had been mentioned at the time of a divorce action in 1908 brought by Vanderbilt's first wife, Mrs. Ellen French Vanderbilt.

More recently, a girl from Virginia who was whip for Vanderbilt's coach horses—which he raced from London to

Brighton—had brought suit against his stable chief. It all seemed most unfortunate.

Many of his friends thought that these unpleasant happenings slowed down the gay parties for which Vanderbilt had been noted since undergraduate days at Yale. No longer could he be seen running his 30,000-dollar racing car over Florida beaches like someone frenzied. Nor was he the same dashing young man who had hired trains and ships to rush home from Japan on learning of the death of his father, Cornelius.

His farewell to New York this trip was simple. Together with friends, the H. Vander Horst Kochs, he and Mrs. Vanderbilt went to the Empire Theater to see *A Celebrated Case,* the first coproduction of David Belasco and Charles Frohman after a rift of almost twenty years.

Others in New York visited the theater that evening too—a ship's captain named Will Turner, for example. He first dined at Luchow's, one of his favorite restaurants, then visited backstage at the New Amsterdam with his pretty niece, Mercedes Desmore. She was appearing in Henry Arthur Jones' *The Lie*.

Justus Forman, forty-one-year-old author-turned-playwright, did not attend the theater, but he did stop at the Knickerbocker Grill at 42nd Street and Broadway, a meeting place for writers, actors, and newspapermen. In addition to admiring the new Maxfield Parrish mural of King Cole behind the bar, he hoped perhaps to elicit a kind word for his *Hyphen* which had opened at the Knickerbocker Theater. It was not a success, yet he comforted himself that it might fare better in Boston, where it would debut at the Hollis next week.

He left early, when few acquaintances appeared, to pack for his sailing on the *Lusitania*. He would travel with Charles Frohman, who still clung to the belief that the younger man could become a successful playwright. Forman himself was somehow less optimistic, despite the backing of the great producer. To tide himself over he had accepted a commitment to write a series of war letters, datelined "France," for the New York *Times*.

In lower Manhattan two young seamen were spending the night in "luxurious if doubtful surroundings." Leslie, eighteen, and his older brother John Clifford Morton, cadets, together with nine shipmates, had jumped the full-rigger *Naiad* rather than face a year's voyage home to England via Australia and perhaps miss the "Great War" entirely. They had already been at sea sixty-three days.

The Mortons, cabled 250 dollars for Second Class fares by their father, quickly consumed their passage in such "exotic" dishes as banana sundaes and assorted frivolities. Along with their other impatient shipmates from the *Naiad*, they now would work their way home on the fast *"Lusy,"* and were happy at the prospect.

Yet 240 miles farther up the Atlantic seaboard, in Boston, a wealthy shoe dealer, about three times the younger Morton's age, decided he was not happy. Edward B. Bowen strode across the living room of his suburban Newton home and lifted the needle arm off the gramophone. The silence which followed "Alexander's Ragtime Band" was welcome.

He picked up the telephone, now that at last he had made

a decision. A talk with a recently arrived London associate had influenced him. He gave the operator the home number of his travel agent.

"Hello," he said, "will you please contact Cunard. We're not sailing tomorrow on the *Lusitania*."

Their luggage was packed. He and Mrs. Bowen had a drawing room reserved on New Haven's midnight sleeper train to New York.

"A feeling grew upon me," he told his friends, "that something was going to happen to the *Lusitania*. I talked it over with Mrs. Bowen and we decided to cancel our passage— although I had an important business engagement in London."

CHAPTER 3

It was warm and barely drizzling in New York, Saturday, May 1, 1915. As on most Saturdays, people would start homeward at noon. But for newspaper editors this Saturday was already set apart. In the morning editions' back pages was a black-bordered, paid insertion:

NOTICE

Travellers intending to embark on the Atlantic voyage are reminded that a state of war exists between Germany and her allies; that the zone of war includes the waters adjacent to the British Isles; that, in accordance with formal notice given by the Imperial German Government, vessels flying the flag of Great Britain or of any of her allies, are liable to destruction in those waters and that travellers sailing in the war zone on ships of Great Britain or her allies do so at their own risk.

Imperial German Embassy
Washington, D.C., April 22, 1915

The notice, which had never appeared before, had been set next to the paid Cunard schedules, advertising today's sailing of the *Lusitania*, the "Fastest and Largest Steamer now in Atlantic Service." The schedule also reported that the

Lusitania would depart from New York again on May 29. At the very bottom of the Cunard notice, "Round The World Tours" were mentioned in prominent type.

The German warning struck a discordant note, surrounded by festive ads from resort hotels in Atlantic City, Connecticut, and the Adirondacks. Some readers missed the Imperial German Embassy's notice, as did many Cunard passengers, especially those in steerage who boarded early. But the editors smelled a brewing story. Not even a cub reporter could miss it.

New York papers called their Washington bureaus. And the correspondents checked at the Embassy. Spokesmen for the Ambassador, Count Johann von Bernstorff, explained the notice had been prepared by a local advertising agency as an "act of friendship" toward the United States, in the interest of protecting its citizens.

Even while the German diplomats in Washington were expressing their concern and fidelity, seasoned reporters, photographers, and newsreel cameramen were converging through the sticky, spring drizzle on Pier 54.

It was no routine sailing, they found. There was more than the usual excitement, noise, and confusion. Some sidewalk photographers were snapping shots of the Cunarder and brazenly hawking them with the assertion, "Last Voyage of the *Lusitania!*"

There was even reason to believe that she would not sail at ten o'clock—though tugboats steamed nervously about the slip and the pilot paced atop the bridge, high as a six-story building. For one thing, forty-one First Class and Cabin Class passengers transferred from the *Cameronia* were arriving at the pier—and their baggage was still somewhere behind them. Most of the forty-one were enormously pleased.

They knew they would be sailing on a larger, faster, safer ship and be in Liverpool nearly four days sooner.

Boarding procedure was slowed to a snail's pace by a kind of Scotland Yard checkup of passengers, visitors, and all baggage. Private detectives and U. S. Immigration representatives mingled with the people on the pier and aboard ship. A purser together with a Cunard agent screened each passenger and his or her luggage, then placed a special chalk mark on it before it went aboard.

Sabotage was a matter of concern.

Nonetheless, Charles P. Sumner, general agent in New York for Cunard, made light of the Embassy's warning.

"You can see how it has affected the public," he told reporters, watching the passengers sweep aboard. He insisted that *no* passage had been canceled.

Alexander Campbell, general manager for John Dewar and sons, London whisky distillers, echoed Sumner's confidence as he went aboard.

"I think it's a lot of tommyrot," he said jovially, adjusting his Homburg, "for any government to do such a thing and it is hard to believe the German Ambassador dictated the advertisement. The *Lusitania* can run away from any submarine the Germans have got and the British Admiralty will see the ship is looked after when she arrives in striking distance of the Irish coast."

Justus Forman hurried on board. His taxi had been caught in an early-morning traffic jam and he had feared he would arrive too late. Apparently he was surprised that there had been a sailing delay, and replied to reporters' questions about his possible submarine fears with a curt,

"I have no time to worry about trifles." He went below to his cabin.

Nor was Forman the only one who filed the U-boat threat in a remote corner of his mind. Sir Hugh Lane, art critic and onetime Director of the Irish National Gallery, could talk of little else but the contract for a portrait by Sargent he had won in a Red Cross rally.

"I already have asked the most beautiful woman in England to pose for the portrait," he told reporters.

George A. Kessler, New York wine merchant distinguished by a bushy black beard, was carrying 2,000,000 dollars in stocks and securities. While he had some transactions in mind which might demand fast financing, he was the kind of person who always preferred to keep his possessions in sight, or close by.

"Much safer this way," he explained to Purser James McCubbin. At the same time McCubbin confided to the "Champagne King" that this was to be his last voyage. He was going to retire to a farm he had just purchased twenty miles from London, near Golders Green.

Unnoticed by the press, Elizabeth Duckworth, red-faced and puffing but refusing help, struggled up the steerage gangway. She held one bulging suitcase before her, the other behind her. Elizabeth was sandwiched in between a group of sweating young Canadians, volunteers going across to the war. There was a sprinkling of uniforms throughout all classes of the ship, while other Reservists had their uniforms with them but were in civilian dress.

Shortly after ten, when moorings should have been cast off, and as cargo and baggage still came aboard, reporters cornered a newsworthy trio on the spacious promenade deck. They were Captain Turner, Vanderbilt, and Charles Frohman, the producer.

Frohman, half-crippled, had to steady himself with a cane.

Several of his plays, in addition to that attended by the Vanderbilts, were currently in production. One of the more popular was *The Shadow,* with Ethel Barrymore, recently moved from Broadway to Boston.

He would see his production of James Barrie's *Rosy Rapture* at the Duke of York Theater in London's Strand and tend to his fall program in England. It was an annual visit, one he usually made in late winter. Frohman occupied the same suite on the *Lusitania* as he had on her sister ship, the *Mauretania.* The latter, like the *Aquitania,* the new queen of the fleet, was now being used as a troop transport.

There was little alike between the three men, either in appearance or professions: Frohman, short, squat, and froglike, always dressed in a dark, double-breasted suit, with a stiff collar and a dark felt hat. Vanderbilt, tall, athletic, with an assurance that often seemed disdain, wore a polka-dot foulard bow tie, a tweed cap, and a single-breasted charcoal gray suit. He sported a pink carnation in his lapel. Turner, short and heavy-set, wore gold braid on his visor and four gold stripes on his sleeve. He looked every bit the British salt he had been for all but eight of his remarkable fifty-nine years.

Questioned about the U-boat threat, Vanderbilt scoffed: "Why should we be afraid of German submarines? We can outdistance any submarine afloat."

Then a reporter asked him if he thought the same luck would hold that had caused him—inexplicably—to cancel his passage on the *Titanic* the night before sailing on her maiden and last voyage, three years before. Vanderbilt smiled faintly.

"Do you think," Captain Turner asked, resting a hand on Vanderbilt's shoulder, "all these people would be booking passage on board the *Lusitania* if they thought she could

be caught by a German submarine? Why, it's the best joke
I've heard in many days, this talk of torpedoing!"

At that both he and the millionaire-sportsman-playboy
were reported as breaking into laughter.

"Germany can concentrate her entire fleet of submarines
on our track," Turner rumbled on, to the reporters, "and we
would elude them. I have never heard of one that could
make twenty-seven knots. We *can* do that, and we are willing
to show them when the opportunity arrives."

He recalled how as skipper of the *Transylvania,* during
the winter, he had successfully outraced U-boats into Queenstown. When one reporter inquired if he might run up the
American flag to deceive submarines, he made no comment.

This subterfuge had been used a few trips earlier on the
Lusitania, when the genial "Paddy" Dow (now sick and
relieved for this voyage by Turner) was in command. The
incident brought a protest from the White House. It was
claimed, in some quarters, that the whole idea had been
proposed by nervous Americans on board.

Turner, a Commodore Captain with Cunard and Number-
Two skipper in the whole impressive fleet, had been the
choice to lead the company's new liners to sea on their
maiden voyages. A wallowing bulky colossus when first
launched, the *Lusitania* needed Turner's firm hand to bridle
her on those early crossings of 1908 and 1909.

He tamed her, broke her in, controlled her vast power.
He made her the fastest thing on the Atlantic—until he
paced the bridge of the newer *Mauretania* in 1910 and beat
his own record. His triumph was the command of the great
Aquitania on her maiden voyage only last year.

When it was pointed out to Frohman that Ellen Terry was
sailing for Britain this morning on an American ship—the

New York—he countered that another actress, Rita Jolivet, was aboard the *Lusitania*. Miss Jolivet had just finished the lead in *What It Means to Be a Woman,* and before that attracted some attention by a four-year run with Otis Skinner in *Kismet*.

The interview was concluded as Frohman limped over to the rail, leaning heavily on his cane. He was very tired, for his fifty-five years, perhaps too tired to tell his interviewers that Ellen Terry had been booked on the *Lusitania* before friends prevailed on her to cancel. The Isadora Duncan troupe of dancers, following her lead, were also aboard the *New York*. Many passengers noticed Frohman standing by the rail, almost morosely, right up to sailing time.

In front of the pier, the newsreels were shooting hundreds of feet of film. Some of the cameramen, like the photo hawkers, thought it a big joke as they explained to their subjects, "We're going to call this 'The *Lusitania*'s Last Voyage.'" Everybody had a good laugh.

They caught the Plamondons stepping from their taxi, used more footage than they had intended while Mr. Plamondon had trouble digging the right change out of his pocket to pay the cabbie. Mrs. Plamondon looked very neat in her flowered straw hat, while young Am appeared exceedingly youthful and natty in his Chesterfield. He wore no hat.

The elder Plamondon had gained the vessel's soft wood decking when a bellboy brought a telegram. He supposed it was some last-minute business communication from his office, until he opened it. He frowned and handed it to his son.

The strangest telegram they had ever read, it was signed *"Morte"* and warned Am's parents not to sail if they valued their lives. They were debating whether to cancel their passage when a friend, David Forgan, president of the First National Bank of Chicago, came aboard to see them off. Now Forgan read it, scratched his head, and discussed it with the Plamondons. Finally he shrugged.

"It's the work of a crank, Charlie," Forgan finally said. "Forget it!"

The Plamondons walked to their cabin, even as the boy continued on his rounds, giving out a few dozen more telegrams, some signed "*Morte*," others with "John Smith," "George Jones," and similar common names.

Vanderbilt received one, which read:

"Have it on definite authority the *Lusitania* is to be torpedoed. You had better cancel passage immediately." He too dismissed it.

One prominent family, the Paul Cromptons, received no telegram. Mr. Crompton, a tall, angular Briton who had been living in Philadelphia, Mrs. Crompton, and their six children were returning to England for the indefinite "duration."

The four sons and two daughters ranged in ages from Stephen, who was seventeen, to little Peter, nine months old. International travel was not new to them. Their father was a director of the Booth Steamship Company, Ltd., and business took him all over the world. Stephen, for example, had been born in Vladivostok; Alberta, who was thirteen, in South America.

The Cromptons were a numerically large example of the nursery-ship character this voyage. There were 129 children, including 39 infants, gurgling, cooing, and crying.

As Cunard officials often said, the *Lusitania* did seem the safest, fastest way to cross the Atlantic—especially for mothers and their children who wanted to get where they were going in a hurry. Surely it was the most comfortable.

It was the most complete ship, too, as any visitor could see. Not only was she equipped with nursery, diet kitchens for babies, a hospital with doctors and nurses, but other wondrous innovations: elevators, kennels for the dogs and other seagoing pets, telephones and electric lights, maids' and valets' rooms, arched doorways, candelabra, inlaid mahogany, damask sofas, Doric columns, fireplaces, grandmother chairs, "roof gardens," and potted palms, blending into an elegant yet homey atmosphere. As a special bonus the *Lusitania*'s owners delighted in boasting she was "unsinkable." Her double-bottom and watertight compartmentation seemed proof enough for that claim.

Yet the lurking hint of tarred decking and rope, paint, engine oil and grease smells, coal smoke, scuppers, bilges, and the ever-present salty aroma of the sea whispered that this, after all, was only a ship.

As a most extraordinary ship, it was often the choice of extraordinary passengers. One such was located by reporters in his comfortable B Deck, portside cabin, chewing on an apple, as he confided:

"I used to be on friendly terms with the Kaiser, but I don't know how I stand with him now, for you know I have written some things he may not have liked . . . if I get through safely and the German Emperor won't see me in Berlin, I'll be patient a while and see him later in St. Helena."

Elbert Hubbard was as eccentric and lovable a character as ever came out of the Midwest. He had tried his hand—successfully—at most everything from selling soap to acting in vaudeville. He was known as "Fra Elbertus," the "Sage"

from East Aurora, New York—where he was the rallying
figure of a cult that had become to many a way of life. His
Roycrofters printed and bound his books and magazines in
such profusion as to be measured best by the pound.

Hubbard's very appearance attracted attention: long hair,
floppy slouch hat, loose, oversized bow tie. He looked like
one of the twelve Apostles in semimodern dress, and his eyes
burned with comparable fervor. As a smart publicist he
wanted it that way.

While best known for his "Message to Garcia," he had
just written a little essay called, "Who Lifted the Lid off
Hell?" It said some very uncomplimentary things about
Kaiser Wilhelm. Even so, as he told reporters, he thought
there might just be a chance that the Kaiser would see him.
Not only could that possibly further the cause of peace but
it would make a good story for his magazine.

Reporters pressed him on the topics of the moment.
"Speaking from a strictly personal point of view," he admitted with a wry chuckle, "I would not mind if they did
sink the ship. It might be a good thing for me. I would
drown with her and that's about the only way I could succeed
in my ambition to get into the Hall of Fame. I'd be a regular
hero and go right to the bottom." He added seriously, "I
shall make no effort to get into the lifeboats unless there is
some spare room."

Accompanying him was his wife, Alice Hubbard.

Shortly after eleven-thirty it became obvious that the liner
would soon sail. The "All Ashore" gongs reverberated
throughout the great length of the ship. Good-by parties
were brought to an abrupt end. The smell of cooking seeped
through the passageways; the first meal aboard was being prepared.

Visitors streamed back down the gangway.

Cargo hatches were secured. Deck crewmen had removed their dressier, starched white sport jackets for turtleneck sweaters and heavy windbreakers more appropriate for sea. They had come alive with a flurry of activity, busy at a thousand little tasks incomprehensible to the landbound.

By noon the pilot's H flag was hoisted from the signal-bridge halyard, the American flag on the narrow stern control bridge. Vertical streamers of assorted alphabet flags were run up on both fore and aft masts. They lent a festive atmosphere, as though it were a cruise ship.

Black smoke belched from the red and black stacks. The gangplanks were pulled creaking onto the pier by long lines of hefty, straining stevedores. Arm-thick hawsers were cast loose from the bollards on shore. Some splashed momentarily into the scummy water of the slip before the seamen drew them up onto the decks.

From deep inside the ship a low hum started which grew into a muffled roar as four steam turbines began to turn. A whirlpool of water frothed at the stern as the four giant propellers began to bite the muddy litter of the Hudson River.

Shortly before twelve-thirty the *Lusitania* was pulling away from her pier.

She gave three mighty blasts of her deep bass horn, which made people clap their hands to their ears. Momentarily the blasts drowned out "Tipperary," which the uniformed ship's band was playing on deck.

On another portion of the same deck, a choral group, the Royal Welsh Male Singers, was solemnly singing "The Star-Spangled Banner."

One or two of those on the dock tossed handfuls of confetti at the towering ship as it slipped out. On the boat deck Elbert Hubbard, who had now swapped his black slouch hat for a sporty gray cap, waved obligingly for the newsreel photographers. Beside him, Alice smiled. Both appeared in gay spirits.

In three minutes the *Lusitania* had backed into midstream. People still waved—handkerchiefs, straw hats, and bright little flags of the Allies that hawkers had sold. But now they had become strangely quiet. Slowly they began to use the handkerchiefs to dab at eyes and cheeks.

For the *Lusitania* suddenly had gone. After all the delays, the doubts, the fears, she had left her pier. She was just as far away from those waving on the dock as though she were already on the other side of the Atlantic Ocean.

Three stubby, high-funneled tugs, the *John Nichols,* the *E. M. Millard,* and the *Lewis K. Pulver,* resembled busy rabbit dogs as they pushed her bow until it was pointing dead downstream, like a long, black arrow. Dwarfed by this giant, they served to magnify her towering mass.

It was always a great sight when the *Lusitania* sailed. People on ferryboats craned their necks as she steamed majestically past the Hoboken docks. Even phlegmatic barge captains looked up with a certain respect in their weather-beaten old eyes. Outside of the Woolworth Building, she was at this moment the biggest thing in New York.

One of those who had come to say good-by started away even before the *Lusitania* quite cleared Pier 54. Am Plamondon was racing across West Street, past the dismal, flatiron-shaped sailor's flophouse, past the smelly packing houses, and up 14th Street to the Seventh Avenue subway. He still felt frustrated at abortive attempts to engage his theater idol, Frohman, in conversation; even though he was aware that the shy Frohman, nicknamed "the Silent Man," never solicited interviews or encouraged fans.

He rode to South Ferry. There he ran out onto the esplanade around the Battery, and the Aquarium. He was just in time.

The big Cunarder—bearing his mother and father along with 157 other Americans—was clearing the Hudson River and sailing out into New York harbor. Already she was picking up speed. The black, boiling ribbon of smoke was beginning to lay flat as it poured from her four funnels. Even the sea gulls were beating their wings in increased tempo to hover just off her graceful schooner stern.

Now the drizzle had stopped and the sun had broken through, warm and bright. Its rays sparkled off the white of *Lusitania*'s superstructure, momentarily glinted as it picked up the big gold lettering of the name on her bows.

Together with other Saturday afternoon strollers and the idlers populating the benches of Battery Park, he watched the ship pass the Statue of Liberty. He knew Staten Island would soon be abeam, then she would sweep through the Narrows.

She grew smaller and smaller. Now, almost all that was left to remind Ambrose or the other watchers on shore that a great liner had passed was a faintly shimmering wake and a nostalgic hint in the air of coal smoke.

Just about this time, in the Biltmore Hotel, Mrs. James H. Brooks, of Bridgeport, Connecticut, was talking over her room telephone with a New York acquaintance. Her husband, who was with the Weed Chain Company, had sailed on the *Lusitania* but had told her not to make the long taxi ride down to see him off.

"Is Jay crazy?" her friend asked. "Didn't he see the notice in the papers this morning, Ruth?"

Ruth Brooks had not. Now she thought of her four boys at home, all under six, and wondered darkly how she and her nurse Miss Hicks would make out if . . . ?

Jay was forty-one and a Maine boy. He had grown up swimming in the icy waters of the Androscoggin, frolicking with logs floating downstream, as other children would with rubber balls in lakes. Somehow this thought made her feel better.

At the Battery, Am walked slowly back to the subway, sweating in his Chesterfield coat. He picked up the evening *Sun* to read on the long ride back to Morningside Heights. Four Zeppelins and a Taube airplane had flown over Lowestoft in Suffolk during the night but had dropped no bombs.

The Royal Navy had bombarded the German U-boat base at Zeebrugge.

The Germans had shelled Dunkirk with long-range guns believed to be forty-two centimeters.

In the less-known South African war theater, a German train had been captured . . . and in the Orient the Japanese had sent an ultimatum to Peking. Everywhere were signs of war.

And much was happening at home: in Philadelphia 3000 women suffragists marched from Washington Square to the Metropolitan House; Mrs. Elizabeth Heck, a widow in East Orange, had turned on the gas jets, bequeathing her landlady one dollar to pay for the gas; Chauncey M. Depew was to be honored at dinner on his eighty-first birthday; New York's Sea Beach subway line had begun full operation; and a police dragnet was out for three dope addicts who had fled Bellevue Hospital in pink pajamas. Advertisements offered diverse commodities from men's spring suits at Lord and Taylor's for $17.50 to "everlasting waves" for madame's hair, and an anti-rattler gadget for Fords.

In Washington, Woodrow Wilson still believed that America could—and should—keep out of the European war.

The paper did not report—because the transatlantic cables had not yet borne the news—that the U. S. tanker *Gulflight* had been torpedoed that morning without warning by a U-boat off the Scilly Islands, in the English Channel.

The tanker was later beached. But three American lives, including that of the captain, had been lost.

CHAPTER 4

The *U-20* slipped her dock at Emden in the early hours of April 30. Her sailing was lonely, like that of sister boats. There were no bands, no girls waving, none to wish "Good luck . . . Come back soon!"

The previous evening Kapitanleutnant Schwieger, recently turned thirty-two, had sat with fellow submarine commanders in a waterfront beer cellar to talk and drink. It was a companionship for which all of his rank became starved in the solitude of their voyages.

This was a far different service from the goose-stepping *"Deutschland Über Alles"*-chorusing Wehrmacht as it trudged down muddy Flanders roads to battle. This was a service of thoughtful and frequently poetic personnel, who almost never "hoched!" the wall pictures of Bismarck or his Prussian progeny.

In submarines there was no glitter. When there was a reward, it was often posthumous.

Hersing, a name which came up tonight as it did when U-boat officers got together, was an exception. In September, even as the Reich Admiralty debated whether the peculiar little *Unterseebooten* were of any value, he had sunk three Royal Navy warships. They were the crusier *Pathfinder,* and the *Triumph* and the *Majestic.* The Kaiser conferred the fatherland's highest honor on Hersing—the Order Pour le Merite.

One month later Droescher, in command of the two-year-old *U-20,* had circled the British Isles on an exploratory cruise. This had never been done before by a U-boat; coupled with Hersing's raid on the fleet, it dramatically rewrote the books on submarine warfare.

In reality, there had been few books and even fewer innovations since Germany bought models from Simon Lake, a naval architect and submarine builder, at the beginning of the century. U-boats were interesting pieces of machinery but regarded by the international clique of battleship admirals with mildly amused tolerance. They were considered about as useless and unpromising as airplanes. On sea, the dreadnought—Mahan said so—on land, the thundering artillery constituted the natural order of warfare.

On another cruise, in January, the *U-20* had sunk three merchant ships in the English Channel. Von Tirpitz was convinced. Here was a brand-new terrible weapon!

It could prey on shipping far more effectively than surface cruisers like the *Emden.* It was an answer to Britain's Home Fleet and the blockade which already hinted at strangulation of Germany. In early 1915 Von Tirpitz had few more than twenty-five U-boats fit for open sea. But he threw them into the fight with a fury never anticipated in Whitehall.

The hate of the Germans had been turned full onto the British. Were it not for them the August and September sweep across Belgium might have seen Prince Wilhelm and his brothers in Paris before the first frost. After storming through places like Verviers, Liége, and Namur, the stubborn block the British helped throw in their path at Mons, Cambrai, and other sectors was a bitter pill. The Londoners had even rushed their double-decker buses across the channel to aid in the defense of Paris!

The U-boat campaign became a balm to the frustrations of the Prussian war machine. The first use of poison gas in late April, against the Canadians at Ypres, was another product of desperation. But it did not break the bloody stalemate on the Western Front.

As Schwieger prepared to sail for his first cruise on the *U-20*, there was little doubt as to his mission. Any ship bearing cargo to sustain the enemy's lifestream must be sunk.

That unarmed merchant vessels should be sent to the bottom without warning, however, or time for crew and passengers to take to the boats, was in violation of the Hague Convention. Considering the Germanic passion for legality, the Kaiser's failure to announce unmistakably his unrestricted submarine warfare until early 1917, two years after he had put it into effect, was at the least surprising.

The *U-20* and another submarine, the *U-27*, had received general sailing orders from headquarters of the *Hochseeflotte*. Both vessels, belonging to the Third Submarine Half-Flotilla, were instructed:

> Large English troop transports expected starting from Liverpool, Bristol (south of Liverpool), Dartmouth . . . get to stations on the fastest possible route around Scotland; hold them as long as supplies permit . . . submarines are to attack transport ships, merchant ships, warships. . . .

As was generally the custom, these were probably accompanied by verbal orders which were never logged.

When Schwieger said good-by to his comrades that evening in Emden, he was tight-lipped, as were all the U-boat commanders. They did not compare orders.

Schwieger's craft was loaded as only a submarine can be. Food presented the greatest problem, and every available inch of space now contained provisions. Vegetables and meats were in the coolest areas, next to the torpedoes and other munitions; sausages were stuffed beside the red grenades, pounds of butter were shoved under two of the bunks, salt and spice had found their way beneath the skipper's bunk—in his own tight cubicle, separated from his control room only by the radio transmitter shack.

Wartime Emden still slept as sailors of the *U-20*, at a shrill whistle, cast off her hawsers. Then the muffled clangor of signal bells sounded below and the diesels began to pound. Like a long gray shark, the U-boat slipped away from the familiar quay and past the towering silhouettes of the High Seas Fleet at mooring. It glided by the bobbing buoys and the lights of the Dutch shore on the port side of the shallow channel, then into the choppier waters of the North Sea.

Dawn was breaking as the submarine cleared the sandy, dreamlike Borkum Reefs, guarding the Dutch and German shorelines, the Wester Ems shoals, and finally Borkum Reef Lightship, twenty-five miles out in the choppy North Sea, the sailors' last reminder of their homeland. The wireless operator calibrated his frequencies with the Borkum station and the ship *Arcona*.

They hove to briefly beside a small fishing trawler. There were "Good Hunting!" wishes from the fishermen as they sent aboard a load of herring. Schwieger's Unterleutnant, signing a receipt which billed the Reichs Admiralty, replied with *"Gott strafe England!"*—then in moments the *U-20* was throbbing her way westward in a cloud of bluish diesel exhaust.

Below decks rang the incongruous sound of dogs yelping—the lingering memory of a Spanish sailing vessel torpedoed on an earlier cruise. The dachshund, named Maria de Malenos after the luckless ship on which she had been mascot, now performed a similar role on the *U-20*. With her were the pups she had whelped, and their sire, the original submarine mascot. The crew joked that it was a German-Spanish *Anschluss*.

Someone took out his accordion; someone else, in another compartment, cranked up the gramophone; there was music. And food—the cook was preparing breakfast of cocoa, bread, and marmalade. On deck they smoked cigars. In the aft torpedo room a gunner hummed *"Die Lorelei"* as with a mother's tenderness he polished, then greased the warhead of a torpedo. It measured exactly twenty-one feet, six inches.

The U-boat, on the surface, but with her red and green running lights shut off, rode up and down just enough so that her crew felt she was at sea. It was a happy boat, and everyone aboard felt a personal devotion to it.

The next afternoon as the *Lusitania*—big enough to carry a flotilla of U-boats on her decks—was churning down Ambrose Channel toward Buoy 1, the *U-20* was raising her first enemy land. Far off the submarine's port bow was a pinpoint of land north of Scotland, between the Orkneys and the Shetlands—Fair Island, familiar to every U-boat crew.

Sighting this lonely outpost meant to her crews that the journey was almost half over. Before long the skipper would give the welcome order to put the helm over to port and head south for the submarine's hunting grounds, off the Irish coast.

There were other signposts, too, for submarines passing through the damp, cold wastes of ocean north of the British Isles: Cape Wrath; and the uninhabited Striant Islands, in the middle of a channel called the Minch; or Nun Rock Lighthouse off the Hebrides and Scotland, on Sule Sherry. U-boat captains made this long detour, preferring to sail far north and then drop south again rather than risk the dread barrage across Dover Straits.

Smaller sea gulls of the North Sea were giving way now to a larger, bolder breed of the Atlantic. The weather was colder too, and the sea and sky grayer-greener and somehow more immense. Sometimes the *U-20* ran on the surface, sometimes just below. She used her antenna-like masts, with heavy steel cables, to protect herself against submarine nets. There were many perils in these waters: vast minefields, destroyers, U-boat decoys, or Q boats, those innocent-appearing trawlers or coastal tramps which attracted U-boats by their very shambling helplessness.

Soon the high reddish-gray cliffs of St. Kilda in the Hebrides appeared. A lonelier Atlantic outpost even than Fair Island, swept by winds and sudden rain squalls, St. Kilda was home to perhaps a hundred persons, living in stone huts like a half-wild race. Their charcoal fires sent thin spirals of white smoke upward, across the island. Even the sea birds inhabiting its cliffs looked different, and called in a strange gutteral cry.

In its one harbor were based patrol boats. The *U-20* hauled past desolate St. Kilda well to seaward.

Then, on May 3, while still in the vicinity of the Hebrides, Kapitanleutnant Schwieger encountered a freighter he judged to be of approximately 2000 tons. He fired one torpedo. It missed. When he noticed the vessel flew the Danish flag, he decided to abandon the attack.

Schwieger was becoming anxious to get on with his mission. Competition was increasingly keen among U-boat commanders, and the *U-23* had just established a challenging record. In its cruise off the southwest and south coasts of Ireland between April 28 and April 30, the *U-23* had sunk the Admiralty collier *Mobile*, two other colliers the *Cherbourg* and *Fulgent*, and the Russian steamer *Svorono*.

There were other sinkings too, from the North Sea westward to St. Kilda and beyond, and south into the Bay of Biscay. Ships of neutrals and belligerents alike watched the steel conning towers rise dripping from the seas—or had first warning when a torpedo brought a crashing end to a world which had seemed secure.

The Danish steamer *Cathay* was sunk during this time in the North Sea. The British trawler *Stratton*, not far away, was sunk by gunfire after its crew had taken to lifeboats. Captain Howard, of the trawler, and his small crew were brought on board the U-boat.

"This isn't one of your newest?" the old fisherman asked with unperturbed interest.

"No," the submarine commander replied, "but don't ask questions. We don't want to hurt your crew, but you were taking food to England. We must stop that."

The Germans had planned to keep the fishermen overnight, putting them ashore toward morning. About 10:00 P.M., a light was observed on the horizon, and the U-boat hastily put the British visitors back in their lifeboat, then submerged and vanished in the darkness.

The trawler *Merrie Islington* was torpedoed off the Irish coast, the steamer *Don* off Scotland. Crew members of the steam trawler *Bennington,* which outran a submarine on April 30, were still congratulating themselves when she was torpedoed off Aberdeenshire, Scotland, and sunk. The crew of another torpedoed and shelled fishing boat, the *Grangewood,* landed on a tiny Orkneys Island inhabited by three people.

The U-boats had much over which to exult. Any schoolboy could understand that neither Britain's merchant and fishing fleets nor those of her friends would last long at this rate.

The *U-20* began to pass through sea scums of flotsam, planking, corking, and other timber and wreckage, testimony to the deadly artistry of sister U-boats.

On May 5, Wednesday, five days after leaving Emden, Schwieger arrived off the Old Head of Kinsale.

CHAPTER 5

On May 1, while the *U-20* was heading out to sea, the *Lusitania* dropped her pilot at Sandy Hook, hauled down the H flag, and felt ahead another few miles through light fog, blowing her horn at intervals. Gradually she throttled back until she was drifting almost without headway.

Shapes materialized out of the murk, soon resolved themselves into three vessels of the British Navy: a converted liner and two warships. A small boat put out from one and splashed alongside. There was a transfer of bulging sacks which appeared to be mail. Then the launch returned to its mother ship and the deck officer of the *Lusitania* signaled "Ahead Full" on the broad dial of the brass telegraph. Bells rang far below as sweating engineers spun huge wheels on the control platform. The ship plowed eastward with a surge of power.

The auxiliary cruiser *Caronia*, once commanded by Captain Turner, the cruisers *Essex* and *Bristol* slipped astern to be engulfed again in the mists. They remained there, patrolling at America's offshore limits.

The *Lusitania* steamed up smoothly to twenty knots. Her

speed had been a constant fascination to the quarter of a million souls she had carried in eight years of North Atlantic shuttling. Soon she outdistanced other liners: the *Cameronia,* now heading—since her sudden requisitioning—for Halifax instead of her scheduled Glasgow; the *New York,* for Liverpool; the *Rotterdam,* for Rotterdam; the *Bergensfjord,* for Bergen: the *Canopic,* for Genoa. All were left behind as the *Lusitania* steamed eastward.

A few passengers desultorily tried on their heavy-stuffed "Boddy's Patent Jackets." Some parents slipped them over the heads of their children who, dressed in the cumbersome life jackets, looked like puffy dolls. Most of the grownups laughed.

At teatime that first afternoon the orchestra played what they thought the people liked, including Carrie Jacobs Bond's "Just a-Wearyin' for You." The forlorn chords served to moisten eyes in the Victorian satinwood music room, especially Elbert Hubbard's, for it was one of his favorite tunes, by his favorite composer. While an effervescent man, he was prone to moments of lachrymose sentiment. He was a homespun, complex, and entirely American species of genius such as neither the passengers on the *Lusitania* nor the world had ever known.

Though the fifty-nine-year-old Sage from East Aurora had crossed the ocean before, he did have some trepidation about the voyage. He'd written to a friend, E. W. Edwards, Saturday morning, "I may meet with a mine or a submarine over there or I may hold friendly converse with a stray bullet in the trenches."

As he did at home, he would make notes or write out observations or even complete articles all day long—and if he came no closer to the Kaiser than the Paris suburbs he would doubtless return with a mass of pennings, ranging in subject from the voyage and its passengers to the Zeppelin raids over London, and the English viewpoint on American neutrality.

After teatime, in his B Deck cabin, he felt a detachment as he so often had in the forests of Erie County, where he could contemplate many things:

. . . his recent pardon from President Wilson, for a conviction two years before in Buffalo Federal Court. He'd been fined 100 dollars on a charge of misuse of the mails, something which Hubbard was sure grew out of a professional grudge. It seemed odd that a man who was known and loved the world over had to ask for a pardon, a man who was on a first-name basis with such people as Teddy Roosevelt, Henry Ford, John D. Rockefeller, Maude Adams, Jim Corbett, and Al Smith.

. . . his sheer mountainous volume of words. Hubbard produced writings with almost unheard-of dispatch. He kept a private secretary with him on most travels, so that no spur-of-the-moment thought would wither unshared. His biographical *Little Journeys* appeared at the assembly-line rate of one a month and encompassed a potpourri of people from Ali Baba to Andrew Carnegie. His magazine *The Philistine* had the unheard-of circulation of a quarter of a million a month, while his "Message to Garcia" alone had sold 40,000,-000 copies.

. . . his following, the 500 or so devoted "Roycrofters," who, in addition to printing and binding of his books, wove rag rugs, manufactured hand-modeled leather goods, beautiful brassware, furniture, and all kinds of pretty little souvenirs.

. . . less pleasant memories, such as his divorce from Bertha

before the turn of the century to marry Alice Moore, an
East Aurora schoolteacher. He rode out the storm of criti-
cism which was bound to ensue, as he carved another motto
over his rustic Roycrofters Inn, *"They Will Talk Anyway."*
He had his own convictions of moral rectitude, faith in a
Supreme Being, even though he was basically an agnostic. He
feared nothing, especially not death.

. . . his love for many other things, for rising at dawn to
chop wood and to ride horseback through the fields and
forests, to compose his writings in the little cabin deep in
those woods. Basically, he had loved people since his youth.
He kept that faith as a cub reporter in Chicago, and even as a
copy writer for a Buffalo soap factory. He went out of his
way to help people if they appeared deserving of help, though
he had devastating barbs ready for those who attacked him.

. . . even war, as far back as the Civil War. He remembered
watching as a boy of nine the soldiers in Union Blue streaming down the hot, dusty road out of Bloomington, Illinois.
Heading South, they would pause at the well for a drink,
then notice the roughly engraved sign nailed over the door
of the weathered frame farmhouse: *"Dr. Hubbard, Physician
and Surgeon."* They would burst into laughter as they sang,
"Old Mother Hubbard," each sure he had first parroted the
quip.

Some called him a "visionary in a reactionary way"; others
a radical. Many considered him the father of modern advertising, while still others thought he had the prose and the
genius of a Shakespeare. And there were also critics who refused even to classify his writings as "literature." One common denominator was above dispute; no one considered
Elbert Hubbard negatively. Even his Buster Brown hair-do
could provoke spirited debate.

A knock on the cabin door signaled to Hubbard that it was evening and time for the cabin steward to check the blackout. Darkening the ship, closing its ports and hatches, had become a routine. Heavy drapes replaced the pillows which passengers had stuffed against the portholes the previous August, when war caught the ship en route to Liverpool.

Now dressed—meaning mostly a clean shirt and another floppy black tie for Elbert—the Hubbards walked over the polished linoleum of the long, hotel-like corridor of B Deck. As they passed the white, red, and blue lights marking exits or fire extinguishers, washrooms, pantries, and other appurtenances of the ship, they held lightly onto the round mahogany railing along either side of the passage. They continued onto the deck, arm-in-arm. Now the stars were bright, the air fresh. They walked several times around the deck, nodding to others as they progressed.

Inside again, they watched the stewards check blackout curtains over the lounge windows, as the cabin stewards had done below. This was largely a precaution against German surface raiders.

The Hubbards proceeded along the ornate corridor to one of the *Lusitania*'s two midships elevators, running six decks down. They alighted at D Deck and entered the white and gold double-deck dining saloon. The high-domed balcony section, seating 500 persons, the modified Corinthian columns, and an immense mahogany sideboard all contributed to the regal aspect.

They passed in the forward part of the saloon a family group which could not fail to attract attention—the Cromptons, seven of them, all but the infant.

As table companions they had a young chap named Ernest

Cowper, war correspondent for the Canadian publication, *Jack Canuck,* and his publisher, Percy W. Rogers, also of Toronto. Hubbard immediately addressed him as Jack and they became good shipboard friends. Jack was bemoaning the fact that his brother Charles, engineer officer on the *Lusitania* until this trip, had been transferred to another liner just before this last sailing from Liverpool.

From the balcony the ship's orchestra played another of Hubbard's favorite tunes, also by Carrie Jacobs Bond, "The End of a Perfect Day." It was "dry, dreary," however, a kind of anathema to such men as "Jay" Brooks, the auto chain salesman from Bridgeport. Every dismal bar of it made him wince.

The evening passed on into night, which was smooth and uneventful for all but the usual sprinkling of first-voyagers. They disagreed among themselves whether the great liner was pitching or rolling, and there was testimony by morning that the *Lusitania* had most certainly given them a rough sleep. The more seasoned travelers simply smiled.

Sunday morning, the second day out, dawned foggy and mild, later clearing. Captain Turner conducted divine services in the main lounge, asked for blessings on the King and all those at sea, and returned to his bridge. He puffed on his pipe and studied the noon position report.

They had logged 501 nautical miles, were south of Nova Scotia; there was a slight swell, a bare breeze. It wasn't much progress for a ship he had once pushed for a record day's run of 617 miles. But with only nineteen boilers, and her battery of 192 furnaces only three-quarters fired, she couldn't do much better.

It seemed to Turner that he had always been racing Cunard ships against those of the Germans: their *Deutschland,* their *Kronprinz Wilhelm,* their *Kaiser Wilhelm II,* or their newer *Kronprinzessin Cecilie.* The *Lusitania* had showed them her stern.

When John Brown built her at Clydebank, Scotland, he blazed marine history by installing four giant steam turbines. The revolutionary engines had never before been tried in so huge a vessel. They made her the most powerful liner afloat. Under a full head of steam her 3,000,000 individual turbine blades could thunder out 70,000 horsepower, driving her forward like a thoroughbred. She boasted many other innovations: electric controls for such operations as steering, closing the 175 watertight compartments, and detecting fire; electric-controlled lifeboat davits for quick launching; she possessed, in fact, the modern equipment needed to make her the fastest, safest ship on the Atlantic.

Before walking below to Sunday dinner at his table in the main dining saloon—reserved for important passengers like Vanderbilt, Frohman, and members of the nobility—Turner was greeted by Staff Captain J. C. Anderson and Chief Engineer Archibald Bryce. He especially liked Bryce, a Cunard veteran of thirty-two years.

At fifty-four, Bryce looked old and leathery, as though tanned from years in the scorching inferno of many engine rooms. The sea, as with Turner, was a tradition in Bryce's family. His father had been engineer aboard one of Cunard's old paddle steamers soon after the company's formation in 1840.

By way of making conversation, Bryce reminded Turner that Kitchener had said the war should really start in May. But Captain Turner had enough reminders of the war, like the Admiralty warnings of two weeks ago:

Confidential Daily Voyage Notice
15th April, 1915, issued under Government War Risks Scheme:

German submarines appear to be operating chiefly off prominent headlands and landfalls. Ships should give prominent
headlands a wide berth.

Confidential memo issued April 16, 1915:

War experience has shown that fast steamers can considerably
reduce the chance of successful surprise submarine attacks by
zigzagging—that is to say, altering the course at short and ir-
regular intervals, say in ten minutes to half an hour. This
course is almost invariably adopted by warships when cruising
in an area known to be infested by submarines. The underwater speed of a submarine is very slow and it is exceedingly
difficult for her to get into position to deliver an attack unless
she can observe and predict the course of the ship attacked.

In other respects, however, Turner felt slightly apart from
the war. The *Lusitania* still could outrun anything the Germans had, except for her capital ships. She carried neutrals,
she was unarmed, with no contraband of consequence, and
although a naval auxiliary she had been rejected for Admiralty duty. Almost anyone, even the captain, would have
reason to feel safe aboard the *Lusitania*.

Turner himself was a Royal Navy reserve commander.
Now, within four years of company retirement, at sixty-three,
he was considered nearly overage, though he remained
strong. The same was true of Archie Bryce. He had been
chief on the *Aquitania*, then transferred from her when she
was requisitioned by the Admiralty.

Turner wished all the "rejects" had as much experience
as himself and Bryce. The Army, Navy, Marines, or the
Royal Air Force took the smart young men, leaving largely

an old crew for the *Lusitania,* or fledglings like Walter Scott Quarrie, from the Isle of Man, twenty-two-year-old ventilating engineer on his first voyage. Bryce had pointed the lad out to Turner as a kind of curiosity, since the popular impression held that only Manx cats came from the Isle of Man.

Something else impressed Turner, as he walked along the bridge, away from Bryce. Quarrie, at twenty-two, was making his first voyage! Turner had been a veteran sailor at that age.

Thwarting his sailor-skipper father's desire that he become a minister, Will ran off to sea as a cabin boy—anything to avoid the clerical life of a "devil dodger," as he put it. His first ship, the bark *Grasmere,* struck a sunken reef during a gale near Belfast and foundered. He stoically refused offers of strong arms and stroked himself across the churning, rock-strewn waters to shore. He could swim like a porpoise.

At thirteen Will had signed on the clipper *White Star* as deckboy, and sailed around the Cape of Good Hope on his first voyage. When the *White Star* arrived at the Guanape Islands, he was surprised to meet his father, the captain of the sailing ship *Queen of the Nations.*

Will shipped over and spent the next year sailing about the world under his father's command. After that he continued his sea education aboard a succession of famous fullriggers, the *War Spirit, Duncraig, Royal Alfred, Prince Frederick, Thunderbolt,* and *Royal George.* Off duty, he read up on navigation, never losing sight of his one ambition—to be a ship's master.

"I was the quickest man aloft in a sailing ship," he would boast, "except for a Greek I once met. And he must have had a monkey for a not very remote ancestor."

Once as second mate on the *Thunderbolt,* bound for Calcutta in the monsoon season, he was fishing for dolphins from the jibboom. A comber came up and swept him over-board.

The first mate tossed him a lifebuoy from the poop deck. It kept him afloat for an hour and twenty minutes until the crew could accomplish the tedious maneuver of changing sails, resetting them, coming up into the wind, and finally launching a rowboat to pick him up. During this time he was surrounded by sharks which he fought off by kicking and shouting; he caught one a sharp uppercut with his right fist.

Will Turner, dripping water, climbed up the rope ladder and onto the forecastle deck of the pitching *Thunderbolt*. The captain, a martinet of the old school, was waiting for him.

"Is that you, Mr. Turner?" he asked, knowing full well the identity of the bedraggled figure who clung to the swaying Jacob's ladder.

"It is, sir."

"Well, you can come aboard and go to your bunk for three days. . . . " Then, methodical as usual, he added kindly, "empty your watch before you turn in . . . or the water may rust the works."

It was one of Will Turner's favorite stories—and he had quite a few.

Turner navigated the globe several times. He became equally familiar with the Roaring Forties below Cape Horn and the halcyon tropical islands in the South Pacific beyond New Zealand.

Though Turner loved sails, he knew that any mariner's future now lay in steam. He reluctantly became junior officer on the Inman liner *Leyland*, and served briefly on her until he joined Cunard in 1878 as third officer of the *Cherbourg*, which steamed from Liverpool to the Mediterranean.

He learned that Cunard would not promote a man to master without a previous command. So Turner, not unhappily, returned temporarily to the billowing canvas and tarred decking. He became master of the clipper bark *Star of the East*.

In 1883, with glowing testimonials from the owners of the vessel, Will Turner walked down the gangplank of sailing ships for the last time. Cunard welcomed him back. Now it had become an increasingly powerful company, with Britain's post office depending heavily upon it for carrying much of its overseas mails. It had directors like proud old E. H. Cunard, whose motto, *"We never lost a life,"* was already becoming famous.

But Turner still faced a long road before he assumed command. Some attributed the delay to his outspoken habits, his tremendous concern for the truth, which put him at a disadvantage alongside more politic captains. Finally, in 1903, he won command of the small steamer *Aleppo,* running in the Mediterranean service.

Then promotion came quickly. It was obvious that this man was a master at shiphandling, lightning turn-arounds in port, as well as a good leader of his crews. In fast succession he rose to larger ships, the *Carpathia, Ivernia, Umbria, Caronia,* and *Carmania.* He had a "feel" for the mammoth creations of steel and iron—a sensitive perception developed from the resilient, far more personal vessels of wood.

He took over the *Lusitania* from his old friend Jim Watt during the crucial early competitive years and drove her with the mailed fist of a Roman charioteer.

Turner became the most famous captain on the whole North Atlantic; hated, yet respected by his German competitors. This sometimes gruff man was loved by his crew, a fact

often considered remarkable by the seafaring set, since he
was as strict a disciplinarian as the best of them.

"If you sail with Will Turner," they said in the pubs of
Liverpool, "you're sailing on a taut ship. . . ."

Passengers agreed.

He fell heir—over more senior captains—to the *Mauretania*,
a slightly faster sister of the *Lusitania;* next, the *Aquitania*.
In addition to being larger than either of its two predecessors,
the latter boasted, of all banal luxuries, a "swimming bath!"

He made shiphandling history one spring morning in New
York by docking the huge liner in nineteen minutes. As captain of the *Mauretania*, in 1912, he saved the crew of the
burning steamship *West Point*. For his difficult maneuvering
to pick up the lifeboats he won the Shipwreck and Humane
Society's Medal.

Will Turner's years had been busy ones . . . he had little
time for puttering around the garden of his home on quiet
De Villiers Avenue, Great Crosby, itself in earshot of the
ship horns on the Mersey. His own family included two sons:
Norman, an officer with the Royal Regiment of Artillery,
fighting somewhere in France; Percy, who had followed his
father to the sea and was now serving in the Merchant Marine. At home he also had pets, a dog and a cat.

As Turner walked along the bridge, Bryce went off to his
quarters to carry out his own considerable responsibilities.
Even in wartime his staff was huge: twenty-four officers. He
had a roster which he often went over under his breath, like
the recitation of some pagan prayer:

"Cockburn, Smith, Duncan, Duncan, Little, Hetherington,
Fairhurst, Cole, Leech, Wylie, Duncan, Jones, Anderson,
Kelly," finally "Quarrie."

He regarded almost every one of them as his children, to

be worried over. He made a point of knowing them all. One in his department, though not a staffer, possessed a charmed life. Frank Tower, an oiler, had swum away from the *Titanic*, and later the *Empress of Ireland* which sank after a collision in the St. Lawrence in 1914 with a loss of 1024 souls.

After lunch this Sunday, Captain Turner looked aft at the crew drilling in the emergency boat. It was always one of two, alternately Number 13 on the starboard, Number 14 on the port. Crew members, to the daily signal from the whistle, donned badges (corresponding to the lifeboat number) and life jackets and jumped into one of the boats. They sat there without attempting to lower the lifeboat. At another signal the crew members all leaped out again and returned to their regular duties.

Chief Officer J. F. Piper reported to Captain Turner that all had been carried out properly. It did not seem necessary for passengers to take part in these drills.

Turner surveyed the smooth, bright seas and puffed contentedly on his pipe. It looked like one of the best crossings of the year. Later, he reflected with somewhat less pleasure, there would be social amenities expected; many distinguished passengers to be entertained in his cabin. There were, of course, Vanderbilt and Frohman, both of whom he knew quite well from other trips, but there were others also.

D. A. Thomas, for example, onetime Liberal Member of Parliament who, they said, reigned benevolently over 50,000 Welsh coal miners.

Lady Mackworth, his young daughter, was a militant suffragette, proud to have spent nights in prison for her activities and beliefs. Here, however, Captain Turner reserved judgment, for he was far less certain of the value of votes for women than he was of the work of someone like Marie de Page. He appreciated what the latter had done for Belgian relief.

Miss Theodate Pope, of Farmington, Connecticut, an acquaintance of Mme de Page. Miss Pope, described as an architect, designer of libraries, Progressive party leader, psychical researcher, was to be the guest in England of Sir Oliver Lodge, the spiritualist. The list did not indicate whether she wore pants but Turner considered that possibility. He thought he had already seen her on deck, tall, striking-looking in a severe way.

There was Commander J. Foster Stackhouse on board, oceanographer, explorer, now planning the International Oceanographic Expedition to the Antarctic for 1916; Albert L. Hopkins, president of the Newport News Shipbuilding and Drydock Company, en route to offer his services in "overcoming" the submarine menace; Major Warren Pearl, former surgeon major with the U. S. Army.

The *Lusitania* always attracted prominent people.

But whether his guests were of the same general cut as himself—Stackhouse, for example—or separated from him by an infinite chasm of sex and thought—as was Miss Pope— Turner had to step aside from his surer role as a navigator when he entertained, and steal time which belonged to his ship. He wondered sometimes if this were not what the prayer book alluded to when it spoke of the "perils of the sea."

CHAPTER 6

The *Lusitania* hammered ahead, averaging hour after hour about twenty knots, which was her maximum under the steam of nineteen boilers. She reached out in her long, easy stride for more and more of the Atlantic. Sometimes she vibrated in short spasms from the brute force of her steam turbines.

Monday morning, May 3, she was off the Grand Banks, taking a gentle beam swell. The sun shone warmly. Many felt foolish for their apprehension of Saturday, especially those few who had mailed farewell letters, before sailing, to their families in Britain.

Shipboard life had assumed a reassuring routine. By 9:00 A.M. all but the second sittings were finished with breakfast. In First Class a robust and varied menu, including meats, challenged the most voracious appetite.

Life and nourishment in Third were more austere. As Cunard occasionally reminded Americans, the *Lusitania* was operated now as a public service, at "no profit" to the line.

Still, it offered the best steerage dining saloon on the Atlantic. It was well illuminated by the light from large square windows. A big room, it was somewhat institution-like, with long tables running beamwise, ten chairs to a side. The chairs themselves were utilitarian and interesting, with bandy steel legs and straight, three-runged wooden backs.

Third Class dining saloon was far forward on D Deck, where any pitching would be felt. The simplified Doric columns were a further reminder of the structural as well as social demarcation between First and Third. They contrasted with the more ornate Corinthian which supported the roof over the higher-fared.

Second Class dining was on the same deck astern, and some complained of the throb and shake of the four huge propellers underneath. Here decorations were planned around an Ionic motif.

By midmorning First Class passengers or their nurses had taken the small children to the nursery on C Deck. Located somewhat amidships, adjoining the children's dining saloon, it afforded the children a smoother ride. But its central position, above Number 2 boiler room, worried some nurses who did not understand the *Lusitania*'s new "thermo-tank" ventilation, meant to insure at least circulating air throughout the ship and a relatively even temperature.

John Crompton, five, spent most of the voyage in First Class nursery. His governess, Dorothy Allen, recent Mount Holyoke graduate, had to give her attention to his nine-month-old brother Peter. Billy Hodges, eight, and his brother Dean, six, were also from Philadelphia. Their father, William Hodges, Sr., thirty-six years old, had been promoted by the Baldwin Locomotive Works to take charge of its business in France. At home he was well known as organist of the Harper Memorial Presbyterian Church.

Yet most of the 129 children aboard were not in First.

Second had the heaviest concentration of youngsters, and accommodated them with a large, corral-like playpen, shepherded by a stewardess. Third had children but no special accommodations—which was especially unfortunate, since here there was another family of six children.

Neighbors in Plainfield, New Jersey, had helped Mrs. John Williams buy passage back to her native England, where she and her children would join her machinist husband, who had preceded them. He hadn't found employment in weeks. There were Edith, Edward, George, Florence, Ethel, and David. Edith, twelve, was able to help with David, who was only four months old.

The private bathrooms of the regal suite on B promenade deck were far roomier and cheerier than Mrs. Williams' entire cabin.

The Walter Mitchells, of Newark, who had never known their Plainfield neighbor, were far more comfortable with their ten-month-old baby in Second. Many mothers, originally booked Third, transferred to the superior comfort of Second when fares were reduced from seventy dollars to fifty dollars for competitive reasons. It was the heart of the nursery, with twenty-one infants-in-arms.

At twelve noon Charles Lauriat, in the First Class smoking lounge, toward the stern, snapped his fingers in disappointment. He had missed the day's betting pool by a few nautical miles. The Lusitania had logged a run of 491 miles. The Boston bookseller, en route to his London offices, wondered what number to pick for the next day's run. He discussed it for a few moments with the noted genealogist, Lothrop Withington, a neighbor of Lauriat's, from nearby Newburyport.

Adult passengers sought distraction by reading books like

Theodore Dreiser's just-published novel *The Financier*.
Theodate Pope's attention was captured by a considerably
less popular book, Henri Bergson's *Matière et Mémoire*, being read aloud by her traveling companion, Edwin Friend.

"It illustrates so wonderfully the common difficulties in
communication," she commented to Friend. An authority on
psychic phenomena, he, like Miss Pope, was from Farmington.
Also en route to the spiritualists' meeting in London, he had
just resigned after a tiff as undersecretary of the American
Society for Psychical Research. He hoped, together with
Theodate, to start another society in England.

People like Theodate—*née* Effie—Pope, who was almost
fifty years old, and Edwin Friend, thirty-five, could not find
companionship with just anyone. Their world was neither a
popular nor a generally understood one. They could be the
object of derision, scorn, or simple incredulity.

On board also were, inevitably, newlyweds. The Stewart
Masons had been married in Boston on April 21. He'd come
from Ipswich, England, to wed his brunette Yankee bride,
Leslie, the daughter of Mr. and Mrs. William Lindsey, of
225 Bay State Road. Her father was a man of many talents;
writer, actor, patron of drama, and millionaire, whose huge
stone mansion brooded over the Charles River in baronial
splendor.

There were younger people returning to live in England,
including twelve-year-old Avis Dolphin, who would stay with
her grandparents while she attended a British school. Her
widowed mother ran a nursing home in St. Thomas, Ontario.
Homesick and miserable with neuralgia, the pert, dark-haired
Avis, who wore big white hair ribbons, like Alice in the
Wonderland book, was befriended by a professor returning
to his home and family in Scotland.

Professor I. B. Stoughton Holbourn had the distinction of being "laird" of a tiny island in the North Sea, variously called Ultima Thule and Foula. There 200 inhabitants were his loyal "subjects." Avis became an honorary "subject" as the two proved inseparable—walking, talking, and reading together.

Holbourn was a traveling lecturer, an authority on classical literature, with the world his classroom. Though mild of manner, he was also a firm and outspoken individual, and was openly critical during the voyage of the lack of lifebelt or lifeboat drills.

He was sitting in the smoking room one afternoon when a gentleman came over and said he wished to speak to him outside. Once on the deck, he explained to the professor that a deputation had been appointed by the male passengers to warn him to stop talking about lifesaving equipment—"It will frighten the lady passengers."

The Scotsman did not argue with the man but obtained a measure of bitter humor from the incident. He secretly dubbed this male deputation the "Ostrich Club."

In Steerage, Elizabeth Duckworth became friendly with Mrs. Alice Scott, of Nelson, England, and her little son, Arthur, who shared her small cabin. The two women proved congenial, and the boy was well behaved.

In Second Class there were 601 passengers—making it the heaviest booked of the accommodations. Because the cabins were so crowded, many spent a great deal of time on deck or in the lounges. One who did so was Archibald Douglas Donald, a Scotch-Canadian in his early twenties who had been working for the Truscon Steel Company in Boston. En route to officers' training at Edinburgh University, he shared a cabin with John Wilson and two others. Wilson, a chemist, had been his roommate at Cambridge. Now the cabin was a cramped jungle of clothes and rumpled bed linen. The ventilating system did little to make things fresh.

In self-defense, Donald embarked on a marathon bridge game, supplementing the ship's formal "whist drives." He paused only to eat, walk the decks, or chat with shipboard acquaintances, like the attractive Grace French. His group started dealing at ten o'clock every morning, took an afternoon intermission "to be with the ladies," then shuffled cards into the night.

His partners were invariably the same. In addition to Wilson, he was joined by another roommate, George Bilbrough, or sometimes by a man known only as "Submarine"—because of his preoccupation with that danger—and an Episcopal minister from Calgary, in western Canada, named H. L. Gwyer, a six-foot-four giant of a man. The Scotch Reverend and his bride of three weeks, Margaret, were homesick for the heather, mild mists, and smell of charcoal fires at evening. But poor Margaret saw precious little of her bridge-playing bridegroom.

The profession of the Reverend Gwyer was variously represented: among others of the faith were the Reverend H. M. Simpson, from British Columbia, and Father Basil W. Maturin, Roman Catholic chaplain at Oxford University and widely read author on religious subjects.

Thirty years before, when the now-elderly Dr. Maturin was an Episcopalian and rector of St. Clement's Church in Philadelphia, he had rivaled Phillips Brooks as a preacher. Theological students read his sermons and treatises as gospel. Even now his speeches were in demand; he had lectured in Boston and had just concluded a Lenten series at the Church of Our Lady of Lourdes in New York.

Bit by bit the clocks of the *Lusitania* were advanced to meet the time in Great Britain, five hours ahead of New York. By Tuesday, May 4, the ship was approaching a half-way meeting of that difference. Though nearly everyone was aware of its passage, time particularly dominated the waking moments of Charles Frohman. Like Elbert Hubbard, he never seemed to find enough of it.

At 5:00 A.M. the roly-poly little man turned restlessly in his bed, blinking his heavy lids. Pain from articular rheumatism, developed after a fall three years before, made him more restless than usual. But lifelong habit and an ever-active brain would have wakened him anyway.

Frohman pondered a dozen new undertakings. Before leaving New York he had dictated the whole of his next season's program of production to his secretary, Peter Mason. Now Frohman's mind jumped ahead to the manuscript of a French play, *La Belle Aventure*, he had brought along. Frohman devoured manuscripts avidly. He always carried a bulging brief case—which happened to be a trade-mark, too, of Hubbard. Habits such as these, or compulsions, coupled with an almost infallible nose for genius in writers and actors alike, were an ingredient of the man's talent which caused critics to label him "starmaker." He was considered, in England as well as America, the greatest theater manager the world had ever known.

Frohman associates knew that he had taken the American theater off the straw circuit and fashioned it into a reputable business. Because of him, it was no longer a sideshow or minstrel. He liked to believe he'd given actors and actresses a new dignity, and security as well.

Hearty voices beyond his window told C.F. the day was beginning. While he breakfasted he wondered why his two

young acquaintances of the German Embassy, Captain Boy-
Ed and Colonel Von Papen, had advised him cryptically not
to sail on the *Lusitania*. There had been dire rumblings all
over town, not confined to the German Club either.

His friends seemed overapprehensive. His whole galaxy,
Ellen Terry, Maude Adams, Julia Sanderson, little Ann Mur-
dock, Otis Skinner, John Drew, William Gillette, even his
good friend Charlie Dillingham; all had been too emotional
and demonstrative for a man of his shy nature. Ethel Barrymore had traveled all the way from Boston, where she had
been playing in *The Shadow* at his Hollis Theater, to say
good-by. Even Paul Potter, one of his oldest business associates, was still talking about U-boats when he saw him off on
Saturday. Could it be they took the German bluster seriously?

C.F. shrugged as he cranked the portable gramophone by
his bed, and the raucous strains of "Alexander's Ragtime
Band" burst forth. He lit up the first of a procession of cigars, pushed back the covers, and called his new valet, William Staunton.

Frohman decided against dressing and going out on deck.
He missed Dr. James Pointon, the ship's regular surgeon. A
younger chap, Dr. J. F. McDermott, had taken Pointon's
place, for the latter was down with rheumatism. Perhaps Mc-
Dermott would come up with a cure for both of them.

Even supported by his "wife," as he'd dubbed his cane,
Frohman moved about the cabin only with difficulty. He
eased himself painfully down on the damask print settee by
the window, where at least he could smell the sea air. Staunton was sent for the inevitable supply of sarsaparilla, ginger
ale, and chestnuts. Frohman's busy mind worked on.

Potter had worried about the financial reverses suffered

by their theater syndicate. There was no disguising the fact that 1914 had been a bad year. But, though he had made theater his business, money meant little to C.F.—"We are developing actors and authors, and that is worthwhile." Oddly enough, for all of his ability to scent out a writer or an actor, even to personally direct the scenes of a play, Frohman never wrote a line and only once appeared in a play.

The public did not always concur with Frohman's choice of artists. Justus Miles Forman, who was aboard, was a case in point. World traveler, dilettante, society playboy, Forman's sentimental novels and magazine stories had met with much more acclaim than his first play, *The Hyphen*. Frohman blamed its failure on war hysteria, since it dealt with German-Americans.

Charley Klein, also on board, was a more successful playwright. Author of *The Lion and the Mouse* and other hits, he would introduce the younger Forman to influential theater brains of London.

Frohman found himself wondering, as he had of late, about the future of the theater. He had voiced the opinion recently that slangy "crook plays" and musical shows might well displace the great drawing-room comedy on the stage and of course the motion picture was taking its toll.

But a man whose syndicate controlled some sixty theaters and had booked upwards of 500 plays in one year in America, England, and France, could hardly waste time in brooding. When the subject of the theater's demise came up, he closed it quickly with the remark, "We won't live to see it."

Three o'clock, then four o'clock—the afternoon fled and with night came a transitory relief from pain. Frohman would have to entertain before the journey was over, but tonight could be spent quietly on his bed, listening to the engine

throb and the swish of water, smelling the ship-sea smells.
He played with a mechanical puzzler and thought about his
fall program—always his program.

The *Lusitania* crossed the imaginary halfway line that
night.

Wednesday, May 5, was as warm and bright as the preceding day. The sea remained smooth and empty of whitecaps.

Marie de Page would avoid Theodate Pope and her world
of spiritualism in favor of conversation with James Houghton of Troy, New York. He was going to assist her husband
in the Belgian hospital at La Panne.

Mme de Page should have preceded Dr. Houghton on this
trip, although the two would have arrived overseas at the
same time. But her desire to outline their important work
during the crossing, as well as to lengthen her tour, caused
her to hurry into the Cunard office at the last minute, beg-
ging for space. The doctor confided that he had signed a new
will Friday night, before sailing. She merely shrugged, explaining that she herself was a happy fatalist.

Among the assistants she hoped to make available for the
doctor was Edith Cavell, in Brussels. That, however, would
involve for Edith a pass through German lines—a task made
difficult by the fact that Miss Cavell was English. Mme de
Page, however, liked to think that doctors and nurses tran-
scended nationalism and the political issues of war.

She reminded Dr. Houghton of how well Matron Cavell
had organized Dr. de Page's clinic and nurses' school at 149
rue de la Culture—the first such institute in all of Belgium.
Nor were there very many more in Europe.

Europe-bound for similar reasons was Dr. Howard Fisher,
of Washington, D.C., to help his English brother-in-law es-

tablish a hospital somewhere in France. With him was a young sister-in-law, Dorothy Conner, a Red Cross volunteer from Medford, Oregon. The two knew Marie de Page, and there had even been talk of their hospital unit joining forces with Dr. de Page at La Panne.

That same day, Wednesday, Dr. Fisher and Dorothy Conner happened to make the acquaintance of the Plamondons. It turned out that Mr. Plamondon knew the doctor's brother, Walter, in Chicago. Charles Plamondon duly noted the meeting in his ever-handy black pocket diary.

Later that afternoon Alfred Vanderbilt was handed a Marconigram advising him that his closest friend and classmate at Yale, Frederick N. Davies, a New York builder, had died suddenly in New York.

And so Wednesday at sea passed, as nearly all—with whatever reasons they had for crossing—became impatient to reach their destinations.

Meanwhile, on Wednesday, off the Old Head of Kinsale, Kapitan Schwieger on the *U-20* was beginning his own activities.

A large, broad-beamed schooner, her patched, dirty sails full to the wind, had been sighted to the east, wallowing a few miles off the coast. The *Earl of Latham* carried a cargo of Irish bacon, eggs, and potatoes for Liverpool, 270 miles to the northeast.

Schwieger hove to alongside, shouted through his megaphone for the crew to abandon. They did so.

A thrill of excitement surged through the U-boat as gunners clambered to man the deck gun. When the men were barely away from the schooner, the *U-20* sent the first projectile into her timbered old sides. A cloud of yellow-brown smoke billowed upward, as the report reverberated over the water.

Eight more rounds exploded into her before she finally flopped over, tipping her masts into the slight waves. She disappeared beneath the surface like a tired, sodden old fish-woman.

That evening the *U-20* fired a torpedo at a 3000-ton Norwegian steamer but missed it. When the ship started after the submarine as though it were attempting to ram, Schwieger gave the order to dive deeper, and continued on his patrol.

During the night as he recharged batteries Schwieger drifted along the coast toward St. George's Channel. The air was cool and fresh, the skies starry.

It was a night, he decided, tailored just for U-boats, and U-boat skippers.

CHAPTER 7

Thursday, May 6, many passengers on B Deck or the next lower, C, were awakened by a new sound which at first frightened them. It was the unmistakable creak of lifeboat davits.

Occasionally there were shouts, and a heavy bump-bump of wood against metal, a weird and abrupt intrusion above the usual background of ship's noises. There had been no blowing of the whistle, no ringing of alarm bells, no frantic raps on cabin doors. The *Lusitania* was steaming along smoothly, on even keel, as she had all night.

Those who were on deck watched the lifeboats being uncovered and swung out over the sides. The keels hung well above the promenade-deck railings, since the rope falls had not actually been lowered, and the boats were still secured to the davits by special chains.

It was a routine precaution. The liner now was within 500 miles of the Irish coast and the war zone.

By breakfast time eleven lifeboats were suspended on each side. Smaller, collapsible-sided wooden boats, were stowed beneath these regular sixty-person heavy boats, so the *Lusi-*

tania had lifesaving equipment for 2605 persons, or a spare margin of more than 600 over those actually on board. There was also an extra quantity of life jackets, including children's, and thirty-five lifebuoys (large cork rings, complete with automatic flares, which would keep one afloat and alive as long as the cold and immersion could be endured).

Captain Turner appreciated precautions of this nature, taken regularly since the *Titanic* disaster only three years before. The *Lusitania*, he felt, had been more than insured against emergencies.

The twenty-two lifeboats hung from their falls as the sun rose. On the starboard side, now facing eastward, shadows stretched across the promenade deck. Later, in the afternoon the shadows from the other eleven boats would slant across the promenade on the port side.

As the lifeboats swayed to the slow, rasping accompaniment of taut ropes, speculation about U-boats filtered back into conversations.

And on May 6, off Kinsale, fog hung on the horizon. Schwieger wrote in his log:

A further advance toward Liverpool, the real field of operations, abandoned for the following reasons—[Points 1, 2, and 3 all concern the fog.] 4. The voyage to the St. George's Channel had consumed so much of our fuel oil that it would be impossible for us to return [to Germany] around the southern end of Ireland if we had now continued to Liverpool. I intend to return as soon as 2/5 of our fuel oil is used up. I intend to avoid, if at all possible, the trip through the North Channel [at the other end of the Irish Sea] on account of the type of patrol service which the *U-20* encountered there on her last trip. 5. Only three torpedoes are still available, of which I wish to save two, if possible, for her return trip.

It is therefore decided to remain south of the entrance into the Bristol Channel to attack steamers until 2/5 of the fuel oil has been used up, especially since chances for favorable attacks are better here and enemy defensive measures less effective than in the Irish Sea near Liverpool. . . .

Soon Schwieger picked out a 6000-ton steamer eighteen miles south of Waterford. It was the Harrison liner *Candidate,* en route to Jamaica, which had just left astern the dark-green painted Coningbeg Lightship.

One torpedo, fired without warning, stopped her dead in her wake. Before she sank, all her crew and passengers got safely away.

Patrolling off Waterford, during the torpedoing, were four armed trawlers. They never sighted the *U-20,* nor Schwieger them. By coincidence another similar-sized Harrison Line ship, the *Centurion,* en route to South Africa, plowed into Schwieger's periscope sights.

Another torpedo, and the *Centurion* went the way of the *Candidate.* Again there were, remarkably, no casualties.

Thursday noon the *Lusitania* had logged 484 nautical miles, averaging slightly over twenty knots.

Turner wasn't satisfied. It had disturbed him from the start to have the *Lusitania* fettered. Now he felt a nagging, inexplicable worry. He sent Archie Bryce below to the chief engineer's more familiar cosmos of heat and grease, steam and metal, unceasing noise and bare-to-the-waist, sweating men. By the netherworld-like glare from the furnaces, the stokers heaved in the coal. Fires roared in the glowing red pits.

At Archie Bryce's instructions his corps of assistant engineers turned wheels, adjusted throttles. The needles on the four drive shafts' rpm gauges quivered, moved slightly beyond 180 . . . held there . . . as though straining to continue. But, like a winded half-miler they couldn't quite put out the extra winning sprint.

Steam pressure on the nineteen hot boilers was almost at a maximum—195 pounds per square inch. Had the *Lusitania* been sailing as a navy ship, without civilian passengers, the engineers might have "taken the wraps off" or tied down the safety valves on the boilers—and trusted to luck they didn't blow.

Generators were humming at about 80 per cent of capacity, or 300 kw Normal.

If the weather held calm, and with the added boost of Gulf Stream offshoots along the Irish coast, the ship might make twenty-one knots that night . . . but not one-fiftieth of a knot over that, Bryce calculated.

He returned topside to tell Turner that the *Lusitania* was now at absolute top cruising speed, under existing steam, volume, and safety conditions. Captain Turner would not order him to take the wraps off.

That evening, Thursday, was the ship's concert, the final social event of the voyage, for the next day everyone would be packing for the arrival at Liverpool. Before the concert there were parties in many rooms, including Frohman's. Guests crowded his suite, among them the actress Rita Jolivet, Charles Klein, Justus Forman, Elbert and Alice Hubbard, Vanderbilt, and Captain Turner himself.

Lott Gadd, the ship's barber, was also invited, and he dropped by for a drink—other guests were impressed by this further indication of Frohman's social democracy.

In their own nearby cabin, and in a much quieter fashion, a couple not of the theater world celebrated. The Charles Plamondons of Chicago marked their thirty-sixth wedding

anniversary with bottles of champagne. In his diary Plamondon noted:

Thursday, May 6, *Lusitania,* 488 miles: Pleasant weather, sunshine all day. Evening concert for sailors' and seamen's homes.

While many of the Frohman party stayed past dinner
time that night, Captain Turner was called away early. A
bellboy handed him a radio message received from the British Admiralty at 7:50 P.M. It read:

Submarines active off south coast of Ireland.

Turner had had no previous warnings, and this message
was additionally disturbing for its very incompleteness. Perhaps some of it had been lost in transmission. He scribbled
a note, requesting a repetition, as he strode back to the
bridge.

At 7:56 P.M. Marconi operator Stewart Hutchinson tapped
out the query in International Morse. The naval wireless
station at Land's End, England, now only about 375 miles
eastward, would have it in seconds.

In a few minutes Captain Turner received the message
again. It was identical with the first.

He stayed on the bridge, in the darkness, as the *Lusitania*
throbbed ahead. The wind against his face was mild, and he
sensed with an old sailor's intuition that he was not far off
land. He could not quite smell it, but he would soon. Even
at night he knew the color and texture of the ocean would
be changing perceptibly as the bottom gradually came up, up,
to meet them, until, in the Mersey there would be barely
enough channel depth for the ship's thirty-seven-and-a-half-
foot draft.

At eight-thirty his radio officer received another, more spe-
cific report which crackled in from the Admiralty:

To all British ships 0005:
Take Liverpool pilot at bar and avoid headlands. Pass harbors
at full speed. Steer mid-channel course. Submarines off Fastnet.

The *Lusitania* acknowledged it and the operator at Land's
End made the notation in his log.

Turner checked with his chief engineer again . . . the four
propellers were still clocking maximum rpm's for available
power, and should show twenty-one knots by next position
report, if fog, which often hung off the Irish coast, wasn't
there to greet them. *"Submarines off Fastnet. . . ."*

The lifeboats had been swung out. Watertight bulkheads
had been closed, with the exception of those with access ways,
cables, machinery, and other control essentials. These latter
could be slammed shut only at the last moment; and when
they were it meant that the vessel's navigation might be
halted altogether.

The engineers confirmed these precautions, while the officer of the deck checked lookout stations. Watches had been
doubled up during the afternoon. Now there were two men,
instead of the usual one, in the crow's-nest, and two in the
bow, or "eyes" of the ship. There were at least two officers
on the bridge at all times, together with quartermasters ordered to keep watch for submarines or whatever was "suspicious" or that remotely suggested a periscope or a periscope's
wake.

Stewards were reminded to see that portholes were tightly
secured and blacked out. All was in order, Turner thought.

He was impressed by the urgency the Admiralty attached
to its "0005" message. It was repeated at intervals a total of
seven times during the night and early morning.

The captain returned to his cabin, lit up his pipe, and

checked, as a matter of habit, his old sextant on his desk. This companion from sailing ship days was almost more precious than the modest 1500 pounds, cash, in his small safe.

He scanned Cunard's familiar blue-typed confidential memorandums. His files were growing thick with them. While the bluish smoke curled upward, he studied them again for hints as to possible courses of action. The situation just might become more critical than he had thought when he sailed from New York.

One document was the Imperial German government's proclamation of February 4, 1915:

> 1. The waters surrounding Great Britain and Ireland, including the whole English Channel, are hereby declared to be war zone. On and after the 18th of February, 1915, every enemy merchant ship found in the said war zone will be destroyed without its being always possible to avert the dangers threatening the crews and passengers on that account.
>
> 2. Even neutral ships are exposed to danger in the war zone, as in view of the misuse of neutral flags ordered on January 31 by the British Government and of the accidents of naval war, it cannot always be avoided to strike even neutral ships in attacks that are directed at enemy ships.
>
> 3. Northward navigation around the Shetland Islands, in the eastern waters of the North Sea and in a strip of not less than thirty miles width along the Netherlands coast is in no danger.
>
> VON POHL
> *Chief of the Admiral Staff of the Navy*

With it was a further amplification, described as a "memorial":

> Just as England declared the whole North Sea between Scotland and Norway to be comprised within the seat of war, so does Germany now declare the waters surrounding Great

Britain and Ireland, including the whole English Channel, to be comprised within the seat of war, and will prevent by all the military means at its disposal all navigation by the enemy in those waters. To this end it will endeavor to destroy, after February 18 next, any merchant vessels of the enemy which present themselves at the seat of war above indicated. Although it may not always be possible to avert the dangers which may menace persons and merchandise. Neutral powers are accordingly forewarned not to continue to entrust their crews, passengers or merchandise to such vessels.

There was a sheaf of British memorandums, interpretations, warnings:

   . . . this is in effect a claim to torpedo at sight, without regard to the safety of the crew or passengers, any merchant vessel under any flag. As it is not in the power of the German Admiralty to maintain any surface craft in these waters, this attack can only be delivered by submarine agency.

By February 10 the British Admiralty was endeavoring to establish procedures to cope with the erupting war at sea:

Vessels navigating in submarine areas should have their boats turned out and fully provisioned. The danger is greatest in the vicinity of ports and off prominent headlands on the coast. Important landfalls in this area should be made after dark whenever possible. So far as is consistent with particular trades and state of tides, vessels should make their ports at dawn.

The *Lusitania* steamed through the night at twenty-one knots. Aside from the short wireless warning, repeated almost monotonously, the night passed as uneventfully as the last five nights at sea. No ships, no lights, nothing suspicious. The lookouts yawned.

Turner retired after leaving instructions to be called in the event of further wireless messages or if for any reason the officer of the watch was in doubt.

Following Thursday's hunting the *U-20* was spending a second peaceful night surfaced, drifting westward just off the Irish coast. Schwieger took position fixes from the lighthouses that winked in friendly fashion. He could estimate within a few yards his shore distance by the flickering yellow glow from the windows of houses.

He encountered none of the naval auxiliaries ordered to patrol the south coast from Fastnet to Waterford. If he had, and had elected to waste a torpedo, they would not have been much of a match—armed, as British editors had remarked in the privacy of their Fleet Street pubs, like a Gilbert and Sullivan navy.

During that same evening, across the Atlantic, in the city rooms of New York newspapers, there were more curious happenings. Mysterious phone callers asked if the steamship *Lusitania,* which had sailed on Saturday, had been torpedoed. Some inquired if her arrival in England had been reported. Others tried merely to raise doubts as to the big vessel's safety.

Many of the calls were from suburban areas in Westchester, Connecticut, Long Island, and New Jersey. All remained anonymous. Editors labeled them as cranks and did not print a word about the night's phenomenon. Not until they compared notes later did they even realize that all papers had been queried. Only then did they wonder if the callers might have had special information about the *Lusitania*—and the U-boats.

Passengers were awakened again early May 7 by another intruding sound—the deep blasting of the fog horn.

After dawn the liner had run into intermittent banks of fog, about seventy-five miles off Cape Clear, at Ireland's southwest tip. Turner, who had slept fitfully, ordered speed reduced to eighteen knots.

This reduction was only partly because of the fog; Turner's other reason was that he wanted to steam through the final miles of the Irish Sea in the dark and arrive at Liverpool Bar about 4:00 A.M. Saturday, May 8. The tide then would be right for Turner to pick up the pilot quickly and nose into the refuge of the Mersey. He might, on the other hand, not stop for the pilot.

Turner breakfasted heartily. It was his same English menu, year in, year out: porridge, kippers, a boiled egg, tea, two scones, with a heaping of marmalade.

By 8:00 A.M. the fog had thickened and Turner signaled for the speed to be reduced again, from eighteen to fifteen knots. These reductions from the twenty-one knots that had been maintained during the night were noticeable to all on board; they could tell by the change in tempo and volume of the deep engine hum.

The ship felt her way forward on a course of 87 degrees East, still blowing her hoarse, throaty horn. Passengers lined the rails and peered into the mist engulfing them.

Now only about 130 miles away, Kapitanleutnant Schwieger, on his *U-20*, was writing in his log:

> Since the fog does not abate, I now resolve upon the return journey, in order to push out into the North Channel in case of good weather.

Even so, he paused a little longer, while his *Unterseeboot* continued to rock gently in the ground swell. The engine crew charged batteries, an off-duty torpedoman switched on the gramophone, the cook sang as he toasted a sausage roll, the dogs yelped, running about the deck, someone laughed at an old joke—the war seemed far away.

Midmorning, the *Lusitania* was passing Fastnet Rock, off Cape Clear, perhaps twenty miles to sea. Because of the fog, it could be only an estimated position. A few passengers, including James Brooks, did think they saw the Fastnet from the boat deck, although Turner himself noted he "did not see it." Nor, for that matter, did he see the submarine that had been reported off the lonely pile of rock.

Shortly after 11:00 A.M. the fog dispersed and the weather became clear and warm. The sea was a flat lake, with a slight ground swell rolling lazily from the coast. Turner ordered a speed of eighteen knots, an increase of three. The course remained unaltered, straight. On the bridge all eyes were strained for the first landfall.

For some minutes nothing was sighted, except a gathering flock of dirty gray sea gulls which flapped alongside the vessel, turning their heads hungrily from side to side. That was the only escort meeting the *Lusitania*, several passengers remarked. There was not even a fishing vessel in view.

At 11:25 A.M. a new Admiralty message was received in the wireless shack:

> Submarine active in southern part of Irish Channel, last heard of twenty miles south of Coningbeg Light Vessel. Make certain *Lusitania* gets this.

Before noon a hazy shadow of land appeared off the port beam. Passengers and ship's officers watched it grow larger and more distinct. Charles Plamondon noted it in his own pocket diary, although he placed the time at 11:00 A.M., a confusion which might have resulted from setting the clocks ahead one hour.

Captain Turner drew on his pipe and squinted.

It must be Brow Head, he finally decided—a medium-sized promontory fifteen miles northwest of Fastnet Rock, almost on the western coast of Ireland. Yet it was confusing. The liner should have passed Fastnet well to seaward and now be on her way up the coast toward Queenstown.

At twelve o'clock a run of only 462 miles since the preceding day was noted. Turner asked Bryce once more to make sure the boilers were ready for full-emergency steam should he give the order for wide-open throttles. Third Officer J. I. Lewis was sent below to inspect the lower decks for secured portholes.

During the same hour Schwieger, who had submerged his U-boat ten or fifteen minutes before and was once again surfaced, was scribbling in his log:

12:50 P.M—a craft with very powerful engines is running above the boat. When the boat came to eleven meters it was seen that the craft that passed above the *U-20* ten minutes before is an English vessel, a small cruiser of old type (*Pelorus* class?) and two funnels. Ran along behind the cruiser so as to attack it when course is changed. The cruiser ran at high speed and on a zigzag course, gradually disappearing in the direction of Queenstown . . .

At twelve-forty, while most passengers lunched, Turner was handed another Admiralty dispatch, which had been relayed through the Valentia wireless in Ireland:

Submarine five miles south of Cape Clear, proceeding west when sighted at 10:00 A.M.

If the land actually had been Brow Head, it would have meant that now the *Lusitania* was past the U-boat, which must be astern, well into the coast.

The fog, Turner thought, had undoubtedly saved them. It was closer than the captain cared—or had expected—to have the enemy.

Chances were, he reasoned, that the U-boat would be on a southwesterly course, en route to intercept traffic on the sea lanes to Ireland, just where the *Lusitania* had been earlier in the morning. This, combined with the Admiralty's earlier location of other U-boats ahead of the *Lusitania* twenty miles south of the Coningbeg Light vessel—between Waterford and St. George's Channel—indicated to Turner that he should move in closer to land. It seemed safer.

He altered course to 67 degrees East, a radical 20-degree change to the north, compared with the course that brought them off the Irish coast. Second Class passengers on C Deck astern watched the bend in the liner's wake. It afforded a sense of comfort to know that they were moving nearer to the protection of land.

Shortly after 1:00 P.M. the bridge watch picked up a good landfall. Turner was quite certain it was Galley Head.

Yet any satisfaction he felt at recognizing this sharp landmark was at once overshadowed by a disturbing realization. Galley Head was forty miles along the coast from Brow Head —obviously he had not covered that distance in the past hour: barely one-third of it, at the most.

If this were Galley Head, the only explanation was that he could not have sighted Brow Head. However, the U-boat reported off Cape Clear by this time must be many miles west of the *Lusitania*.

The *Lusitania* was held on 67 degrees East, steady.

The Irish coastline gradually assumed a clear, definite shape. By 1:30 P.M., trees, rooftops, and church steeples could be discerned, slowly sweeping past, to port. There was a sense of relief that the crossing had been made safely. The days spent recently on the lonely Atlantic were already becoming a memory.

Yet around the liner the flat, blue-green waters remained empty of other shipping or warships of any description. This puzzled Turner, Anderson, Bryce, and the other ranking officers. They had been shown the Admiralty charts designating this as War Area XXI—starting at the Blaskets on the west coast, just above Dingle Bay, and extending all the way along the south coast to Carnsore Point, at the entrance to St. George's Channel and the Irish Sea. The Irish Coast Patrol, consisting, in addition to some old cruisers and destroyers, of four armed yachts and sixteen armed trawlers, was charged with the protection of Area XXI. Yet where were they? Where was any one of them?

The defense of Britain's principal lifeline was admittedly weak. The Mediterranean Fleet was being bled in the ill-starred Dardanelles campaign. The Grand Fleet was guarding home waters against the Kaiser's High Seas Fleet which glowered with exceptional menace from its ports just across the North Sea.

Turner had been advised of the Irish Coast Patrol. He did not know that a slight acquaintance, Rear Admiral H. L. A. Hood, had just arrived in Queenstown to take command. Curiously enough, guarding these all-important sea lanes had been assigned him as a sort of wrist slap for a "not wholly effective" job in organizing the Dover patrol.

At 1:40 P.M. Turner picked up a landmark as familiar as his pipe or the roses over his front door at Great Crosby—

the Old Head of Kinsale. Mariners had taken bearings on the loaflike headland for centuries.

He knew where he was. He also knew that he should avoid the headlands. He knew, too, that if he followed Admiralty doctrine he should pass ports at full speed. On his present course he would be abeam of Queenstown and busy Cork Harbor in less than two hours.

Yet, if he increased speed, he would arrive at Liverpool Bar ahead of full tide. That could mean dangerous circling outside the Mersey for several hours.

He was aware that zigzagging was accepted procedure in infested waters. But it was his impression that zigzag instructions applied only *after* a submarine had been sighted. Moreover, if he zigzagged he could not firmly establish his position. Having already mistaken some other piece of land for Brow Head, he now wanted not only a good, long look at Kinsale but the *Lusitania*'s position off it established beyond doubt.

He knew he should steer mid-channel, to comply with another element in the complex Admiralty instructions before him. But the approaches to St. George's along this coast were wide. A mid-channel course might put him directly in the path of the submarines reported ahead, off Waterford.

What Captain Turner did not know, for the very reason the Admiralty had not advised him, was that a total of twenty-three merchant vessels had been torpedoed in the waters of his general steaming area since he sailed from New York on Saturday.

Not a single escort ship, not even an auxiliary, was in sight. By its very presence so much as one armed trawler might have eased Turner's dilemma.

Yet one thing was above question. He must change course

back to the east, lest he run hard aground on the sandy Saltes
Islands, farther along the coast, just westward of St. George's
Channel.

At 1:45 P.M., the helmsman swung the *Lusitania* again to
the original 87 degrees East.

With heavy hearts passengers watched the liner veer away
from the green, friendly-looking land.

Several minutes later Seaman Thomas Mahoney, on the
fo'csle watch, spotted something "that appeared suspicious."
It was an object, two points on the starboard bow, "conical
in shape." He reported it to the officer of the watch and there
was "a little commotion" on the bridge over what it might
be. The liner pushed past it; the object, a buoy, was harm-
less.

Now William Thomas Turner, in full command, felt
worried and alone. His loneliness was that which only genera-
tions of skippers could truly understand.

To him fell the same character of responsibility that others
before him had faced since the days of sailing ships—with
so many souls in his trust, should a skipper reef in before the
gale and try this tack, or haul about for another one? In
which course was salvation, in which total destruction? Warfare added its own mortal confusion to a veteran mariner's
daily demands for decision.

Turner's loneliness was accentuated by the fact that he
could not—or, in pride, would not—ask advice, not even of a
staff captain, like Anderson. You commanded the queens of
a company's fleet, Will Turner knew, because *you* were supposed to possess the superior judgment for just such moments as this. Where Admiralty procedures and warnings left
off, *you* were supposed to pick up.

After considering quickly again the alternatives before

him, Turner made up his mind. He ordered a four-point bearing on the Old Head of Kinsale. The *Lusitania* would have to remain on a completely straight, undeviating course during the forty minutes required. Speed must be held constant, unchanged by not even a fraction of a knot.

But when the bearing was finished, if not before, Turner would be certain of one thing—he would know just where the *Lusitania* was.

Another officer, Kapitanleutnant Schwieger, was already certain where the "large passenger steamer" was. He never moved his periscope off her since first she steamed over the horizon. Now her captain had obligingly maneuvered her into position for a perfect shot.

"Torpedoes cleared . . ."

CHAPTER 8

On the *Lusitania* Albert A. Bestic, junior third officer, commenced his four-point bearing on the Old Head of Kinsale. It was 1:50 P.M. by the clock on the bridge.

Ten minutes later Bestic—whom Captain Turner always called "Bissitt"—was relieved and went to his cabin. He had barely sat down at his small desk to bring his log up to date when the ship's baggage master appeared at the door.

"The men are waiting for you in the baggage room, sir," he informed Bestic. It was a regulation in Cunard that an officer must be present during the tedious process of bringing heavy baggage up on a cargo lift. Three thousand sacks of mail, the first cargo to be unloaded, also had to be brought up from the mail hold.

Bestic stood up, then remembered that he was wearing a new uniform, just purchased in New York. Even for the supervising officer, baggage moving was a dirty job. Bestic told the baggage master he would be right along, and quickly began to change uniforms.

The clock over his desk read 2:09 P.M. . . . and he knew he had to hurry.

While Bestic and most other officers prepared for their afternoon duties; many passengers were walking the sunlit decks; or lying on deck chairs; others were resting or packing in their cabins or finishing second-sitting lunch.

Robert J. Timmins and his cabin mate Ralph Moodie, British cotton dealers who made their headquarters in Gainesville, Texas, were still eating heartily. They had worked up a sweat playing medicine ball, then cooled off with a round of drinks. Now, as the orchestra played the "Blue Danube," they were relaxed and content.

They laughed as they remembered the Greek sea captain who had strapped on his lifebelt the evening before, clambered into one of the gently swinging life boats, and slept there all night. No amount of persuasion could make the adamant Greek move. Timmins thought it was the funniest sight he had ever seen. He ordered a second dish of ice cream.

"We've got time, ' he said, leaning back, wiping perspiration from his cheeks which the laughter had started anew. He was a big, heavy man.

Moodie glanced at his wrist watch and agreed there was plenty of time . . . after all, it was only a few minutes past two.

Archibald Donald, in Second Class dining saloon, was also finishing lunch, with Gwyer, his wife Margaret, and another table companion, Miss Lorna Pavey of Saskatchewan.

Donald watched Lorna eat a grapefruit, and somehow found it funny. He teased her about her choice of dessert, and finally the Gwyers joined in. Lorna, a pretty, round-faced young lady en route to serve with the Red Cross, seemed embarrassed.

Herbert Ehrhardt was also finishing lunch. An English-

man, he had been studying for his M.A. in chemistry at the
University of Toronto and was now on his way home for the
summer, earlier than usual since wartime semesters had been
foreshortened in Canada.

During the voyage he had been a kind of Pied Piper: six
or seven young children had affixed themselves to him and
would not leave him alone. Fortunately a girl of sixteen had
lent a helping hand. This role somehow amused his two
brothers and the other young man who shared his cabin.

Theodate Pope and her fellow psychicalist Edwin Friend
were experiencing one of their rare moments of levity, occa-
sioned not by a grapefruit but by a dish of ice cream. It had
been ordered by a youthful Englishman seated across from
them. His ice cream had arrived but the waiter had neg-
lected to bring a spoon.

The others laughed, then commented on how slowly the
ship was running. Theodate believed the engines had
stopped. She and Friend left the table, as the orchestra still
drummed the "Blue Danube." On the way out they encountered Oliver P. Bernard, a young English acquaintance, scenic
director of the Boston Opera House and Covent Garden in
London. He was paying his wine bill and turned to speak to
them as they passed.

Theodate and Friend continued to B Deck and leaned
over the railing of the starboard side. They agreed the sea
was a "marvelous blue" as well as "very dazzling in the sunlight."

They continued walking, turning the corner at the aft end
of the deck, around the heavy paneled smoking room, where
the clock already read past 2:09 P.M.

Oliver Bernard too, had the feeling the ship had stopped.
On reaching the almost-deserted port promenade, he became

irritated by the slow progress of the ship. Then he continued round to starboard and settled aft in the veranda café, staring out over the sparkling sea.

He was lost in reverie when something on the sea "impinged on my mental focus." His mind "twanged" like a door slammed and he came back to the reality of the ship.

Dorothy Conner and Dr. Fisher had arrived very late for lunch. Now they were sipping coffee with their table companions, Lady Margaret Mackworth, the young suffragette, and her wealthy, former Liberal M.P. father, D. A. Thomas. The latter had been teasing Dorothy, a Red Cross volunteer, about a remark she had made that morning. She had found the fog depressing and ominous.

"It's been such a dull, dreary, stupid trip," she confessed. "I can't help hoping that we get some sort of thrill going up the channel."

Now Lady Mackworth and her father excused themselves, leaving the doctor and his sister-in-law almost alone in the plush magnificence of First Class dining saloon.

The Elbert Hubbards had been moving around the *Lusitania* at a brisk, almost excited pace ever since land was sighted. "Bill" Kaiser seemed so much nearer now.

Hubbard's humor continued unsuppressed. He was talking with the Boston bookseller, Charles Lauriat, on the promenade deck forward on the port side. The author of "Who Lifted the Lid Off Hell?" was still intrigued with the idea of seeing the Kaiser. He reiterated, with a twinkle in his eye, that he was not certain of his welcome in Germany.

And on the Marconi deck on the starboard side, James Brooks, of Bridgeport, was busy talking with an Englishman and his wife. The man had been representing his firm in Chicago.

Below them, on the promenade, Mrs. Florence Padley, traveling from her home in Vancouver to Liverpool for a visit, was resting in a deck chair. Someone in front of her remarked, "There's a porpoise." Mrs. Padley jumped up to look.

At the same time some persons were still dining in Third Class. Among them was Elizabeth Duckworth. Her acquaintance of the voyage, Alice Scott, had just started back for the cabin with her small son Arthur.

Many other persons, in their cabins, were in the process of putting infants to bed. Rattles and toys had been set aside and only the litter of food hinted of feeding time just passed.

During the sixty seconds between 2:09 P.M. and 2:10 P.M. on May 7, 1915, an era ended . . . and a new one began.

For in the *U-20* came the electrifying announcement:

"Torpedo ready!"

Schwieger, his eye tight against his periscope, gave the final corrections to the wheelman controlling the finlike hydroplanes and the rudder:

"Up, down! Up a little! One degree right . . . meet it!"

No time even to study the depth-gauge meter.

"Fire!"

A hiss of air in the forward torpedo room, a quick shudder as the U-boat was suddenly lightened by almost a ton.

Kapitanleutnant Schwieger reported:

"Clean bow shot from 700 meters range (G torpedo three meters depth adjustment) cutting angle 90 degrees. Estimated speed twenty-two sea miles."

On watch as extra lookout on the starboard side of the *Lusitania*'s forecastle, Seaman Leslie Morton suddenly saw the telltale white streak in the water arrowing toward his ship. From the fo'csle head he shouted through a megaphone, to the bridge:

"Torpedoes coming on the starboard side!"

A split second later, from his lofty perch in the crow's-nest, Able Seaman Thomas Quinn sighted the same deadly wake and reached for the intercommunication telephone.

Second Officer P. Hefford heard Morton's call and repeated it:

"There is a torpedo coming, sir!"

Captain Turner, studying the Old Head of Kinsale from the port side of the lower bridge, looked up. Now the torpedo was so close that he could see its foamy wake from the far side of the great ship's eighty-eight-foot beam, where he stood.

He took one step toward the center of the bridge and the man at the helm.

At 2:10 P.M. (3:10 P.M. by German clock settings) U-boat Commander Schwieger continued in his log:

> . . . shot hits starboard side right behind bridge. An unusually heavy detonation follows with a very strong explosion cloud (high in the air over first smokestack). Added to the explosion of the torpedo there must have been a second explosion (boiler, coal, or powder). The superstructure over point struck and the high bridge are rent asunder and fire breaks out and envelopes the high bridge. The ship stops immediately and quickly heels to starboard. At the same time diving deeper at the bow. . . .

CHAPTER 9

On the *Lusitania* no one was in full agreement as to where the torpedo had hit, or even how many had been fired. There was also a general, rather remarkable absence of surprise that it happened.

Captain Turner, who had started from the port side, never reached the starboard bridge wing before the torpedo struck the seven-eighths-inch-thick steel sides of the ship. He felt the vessel reel under a terrific explosion he believed to be in the starboard stokeholds.

The decks seemed to rise underfoot, then settle. A column of steam and water geysered noisily as coal and wood and steel splinters were hurled 160 feet above the radio antenna and fell in an avalanche upon the upper deck. The 32,000-ton speed queen faltered and listed to starboard.

Turner gave the order to put the helm over . . . the land loomed so closely. Could he beach her?

The hissing from far below in the *Lusitania*'s blasted vitals gave the answer—steam pipes had ruptured. As they burst they sounded, to some, like the "rattling of a Maxim gun."

She was still going at almost eighteen knots, because of

her great momentum. But the engine telegraph would not work . . . Lights were flickering as generators threatened to fail.

It was 2:10 P.M. A welter of activity took place on the stricken ship during the next few minutes.

Marconi Operator Robert Leith sprinted out of the Second Class dining room, through the passageways, and up the ladder to relieve his junior assistant at the key. Within seconds he had tapped out, almost reflexively:

Come at once, big list, 10 miles south Old Head Kinsale.

He repeated it, and again, followed by the call letters, MSU, noting all the while that the ship's electric power was weakening. He eyed the emergency dynamo in a corner of his radio shack.

Senior Second Engineer Andrew Cockburn, on an upper grating of the many-storied engine room, realized at once that the angel of death had spared him. After the deafening concussion and blinding flash of light in his greasy, steamy domain, there was blackness, escaping steam. The air became heavy with acrid coal smoke. He thought a boiler had exploded.

As he held onto a steel railing and started to examine himself for injuries, he could hear the water gushing into the engine room, in a volume that he quickly concluded would be fatal. It was apparent to him that there had been a great deal of internal damage to the ship.

He estimated, from his position—and from the very fact of his continued existence—that the damage had been centered in Numbers 1 and 2 boiler rooms, which now were probably flooded. He suspected that one or both coal bunkers had also been blown open.

Cockburn had last seen Chief Engineer Archibald Bryce, and many others of the large engineering staff, in that area.

Senior Third Engineer George Little, on a lower level in the same below-waterline area, watched steam-pressure gauges sink from 190 to 50 pounds, like the certain, slow sigh of a dying person.

Far above him, on the narrow Marconi deck in the highest part of the superstructure, "Jay" Brooks had seen the torpedo when it was about 100 feet away, just forward of his position. Mechanically, it fascinated him.

"Torpedo!" he shouted. As he did so, he grasped the little rail of the Marconi deck with both hands and leaned over, balancing himself with one foot off the deck and up in the air. He saw the torpedo vanish into the side of the *Lusitania*. But nothing happened.

He waited, frozen in position like a ballet dancer.

Snug inside the vitals of the liner, the delayed fuse went off. The jolt and shock to Brooks was more stunning than noisy.

Next, the large ventilator nearest the bridge on his side, and directly under Number 1 funnel, geysered steam, water, coal, smoke, and other debris. Brooks unfroze and took two steps toward the Marconi house and the gushing ventilator. It was his undoing.

Although he was twenty-five feet or so aft of the ventilator, the debris fell back on the deck. The water knocked him flat on his face, while the steam choked him. He had the horrible sensation he was going to suffocate.

Then the wind blew the steam away, leaving him covered with soot. He could breathe again, but he was frightened. He leaped to his feet, ran across the Marconi deck and down on the port side to the boat deck. He continued aft and into the smoking room via its rear door. It was already deserted.

He was still seized with panic and could not stop. He went out the starboard side of the smoking room, watched some begrimed stokers emerge wearing what looked like athletic sweat shirts, then started forward.

There did not appear to be many people on deck. He had the impression that others were less concerned than he. He kept on toward the bridge.

On the promenade deck, Lauriat had perceived the impact as a "heavy, rather muffled sound." The ship had trembled before the second explosion, which sounded to Lauriat more like a boiler going in the engine room. He too witnessed the shower of coal, steam, and debris and within seconds heard the fall of gratings and other wreckage onto the superstructure and decks. Soot speckled his white shirt.

Lauriat, a summer sailor in Massachusetts waters, had no doubt that the *Lusitania* was seriously hurt. Because of her list to starboard and almost immediate pitch by the head he reasoned she was going down.

Then she steadied, started to right herself, and he momentarily changed his mind. It looked as though she might stay afloat, and it gave him a lulling sense of security, as it did to almost all others aboard.

He suggested to the Hubbards that they go to their cabins for life jackets. Their B Deck stateroom was at the foot of the main companionway, and Lauriat knew they could run down and back in no time—even considering the list.

But Hubbard just stood there "affectionately" holding his arm around Alice's waist, with a strange lack of inclination to move.

"If you don't care to come," Lauriat declared, "stay here and I will get them for you."

The Boston bookseller hurried below. As he moved down the companionway he changed his mind again. The list *was* bad—he was going to have to swim for it. But somehow the prospect did not frighten him.

Lady Mackworth had heard the explosion too; it sounded "dull, thud-like, not very loud," to her. She had previously made up her mind that if anything happened she'd go straight for her lifebelt, then to the boat deck. Now, while her father Thomas stood looking out of a porthole, she ran up the stairs, which were already at a strange, unfamiliar angle.

Her cabin was on B Deck, well down a passage. Halfway, she approached a stewardess, who manifested amazing calm even though her starched cap was at an angle which would have been comic under other circumstances. Both Lady Mackworth and the stewardess were clutching the railing, since the ship now was heeled acutely. It was almost necessary to walk in the angle formed by the deck and the wall, or bulkhead. The two women collided, then stood there making "polite" apologies to each other until they realized they were wasting precious seconds. They laughed at the utter absurdity of their manners . . . and hurried on.

Reaching her cabin, Lady Mackworth pulled her lifebelt off its wall hook. Moving out again into the passage, she ducked into her father's cabin long enough to grab his lifebelt, and then continued down the passageway.

People crowded it, looking for their own belts. She raced up the companionway to A Deck, the boat deck, and to the port side, the highest from the water. She had the idea it would be safer, since it was also the side farthest from the submarine.

There in the sunshine stood Dr. Fisher and Miss Conner.

Lady Mackworth asked if she might stay beside them until she caught sight of her father. To Dorothy Conner she commented, "Well, I guess you've had your thrill."

Florence Padley approached the elevator bank on the promenade, with the thought of going below for her lifebelt. When she had stepped to the rail to see the "porpoise," she had realized at once what it was.

"No, it's a torpedo," she cried and hurried toward the elevator.

As she neared the lift she saw one of them "go down in a rush." She decided that her D Deck cabin was too far below, so she fled up the stairs toward the boat deck instead. She lost a shoe in her haste.

Halfway around the corner of the promenade deck outside of the smoking room Theodate Pope and Edwin Friend paused, looked at each other. The sound of the explosion had been clear and unmistakable. When water and timbers "flew" past the deck, Friend struck his fist in his hand and exclaimed, "By Jove, they've got us!"

Just as the two rushed into a small corridor, the ship listed so heavily to starboard that both were thrown against the wall. But they missed the shower of soot which cascaded onto the deck.

They recovered their balance and started toward the boat deck, where they had previously arranged with other friends to meet in the event of just such an emergency.

The deck suddenly became crowded with people. Two women walked by crying in a "pitifully weak" way. An officer shouted orders to stop lowering the boats and told everyone to go down to B Deck since the lifeboats were hanging at that level.

No one paid much attention to him.

The spiritualist from Farmington waited a second with a kind of weary resignation before obeying the order. She paused only a moment to watch a boatful of men and women being lowered.

The ship was still plunging ahead, erratically. Theodate Pope wondered, as did the other passengers, why in the world the captain didn't stop the *Lusitania*.

In the Second Class dining saloon there had been no sound of explosion, only a shattering of glass. To Archibald Donald, on his way to fight in the war, it sounded like someone had fallen through a "glass house."

Most diners had stood up as in a single motion. The lights soon flickered out. There was some screaming and then several thuds as a few persons fell to the deck. The towering Reverend Gwyer touched Donald on the shoulder and suggested:

"Let us quieten the people." It was the tone of voice he might have used to preface a prayer."

The two moved quickly to the entrance door and shouted at the top of their voices that everything would be all right, there was no need for hurrying. Neither man really believed it, but it had the desired effect.

The diners, even those who had at first seemed half hysterical or half paralyzed with fright, filed out of the room like a "regiment of soldiers." There was no trampling; everybody moved quickly, but nobody pushed or shoved.

As they left, the listing became worse and more plates, cups, saucers, and silver crashed onto the hard decking. To some the sound was noisier than the bursting of the torpedo. Several mistook it for exploding ammunition.

One woman fainted as she passed Donald. Her husband picked her up around the shoulders while Archie took hold of her feet. They carried her up the stairs. It was no easy task since the stairs were now at a difficult angle for climbing.

Donald's first sight when he came out on Second Class deck, astern, was that of smudged stokers and cooks emerging from their stations. He paused as he heard the noise overhead of boat falls running through davits.

He was fascinated by the sight of the crewmen. In their apparent terror they seemed "a wild lot."

Herbert Ehrhardt, the student, found other tasks for himself as Donald and Gwyer took command of the Second Class diners. He noticed many portholes were open. Together with Wilson, Donald's roommate, several other men, and some of the stewards, he closed them and dogged them down tightly with their heavy brass bolts.

It occurred to him that this might help in saving the ship. He remarked to himself on how the room had emptied without any panic, and then decided he'd better get his life jacket, particularly since there was a smell of smoke.

His cabin was next to the stairs, presenting no problem of being trapped in the corridors if the great ship foundered. However, once in his topsy-turvy cabin, he found that someone had already taken his life jacket. This did not bother him. Ehrhardt had always been an exceptionally strong swimmer and had previously been dunked while fully clothed. Without reasoning it through, it seemed in no way preposterous that he would simply swim to Ireland, with or without a jacket.

Before leaving his cabin, he transferred money from his locked suitcase to his pocket. It represented part of his pay as a demonstrator in the University of Toronto's chemistry department, and he was extremely proud of the modest sum, for it was the first he had earned.

On deck, Ehrhardt found people waiting "calmly" for lifeboats to be launched. He encountered the oldest girl of the
children who had befriended him, and found her very distressed because her brother had somehow become separated
from the rest of the family. The family consisted, in addition
to her and her brother, of her mother, father, and younger
sister.

Ehrhardt went looking for the boy.

He could perceive a latent but gradually growing fear
within himself. At the same time there was an increasing
determination not to let that fear cloud his common sense
or to cause him to do "anything which I would regret or
blame myself for in later life."

In the deeper recesses of steerage there had been a "terrible crash" when the torpedo struck. Elizabeth Duckworth,
walking with the Scotts, mother and son, felt the ship shake
"from stem to stern."

They rushed to their forward deck and were told there
was a "gaping hole" in her side, that she was indeed going
to sink by that very bow near which they stood. It seemed
that the green sea had but a short space to roll over the
winches, chains, and cables on the well deck before it came
and swallowed them too, even though they were on a slightly
higher level.

The two women, brushing off the cinders which had mys-
teriously rained on their blouses, were suddenly struck by
the fact they were "helpless in midocean." For a moment
Elizabeth watched almost numbly as others rushed for the
lifeboats.

Then panic gripped her. With Alice Scott and little Arthur
Scott, she started swiftly up the forward mast's rigging, struggling, clutching at the tarred ropes.

An officer clambered more nimbly after the trio and said in a calm voice to come down. He assured them there was a lifeboat ready, on the promenade deck, which was the abandon-ship deck under normal procedure. A passenger should step from the railing of that deck right into the lowered boat.

Elizabeth told Arthur Scott to slide down the rope ladder— he was already halfway up—and she would catch him. But he was "afraid and scared."

"Come on, you will be lost!" she called.

Arthur summoned his courage and slid down. But Elizabeth missed him, and the boy landed on his back with a thud. It knocked the wind out of him and he lay on the wood decking as though dead. He came to in a few seconds, however, and the three hurried on toward the lifeboat. Another ship's officer called: "We can get the little boy in, but we can't get you in!"

"All right, get him in," Elizabeth answered, starting toward another boat. The noise of a gathering storm of voices now compounded her own confusion.

There wasn't room in that one either, and the sailor beside it pointed to the last one down the long line of swaying starboard-side boats and to the milling, sometimes crying people. Elizabeth stumbled and fell onto the deck.

An officer picked her up and dragged her toward the last boat.

Robert Wiemann, First Class saloon waiter, had been standing behind his table, waiting for his last diner to finish lunch, when the torpedo struck. It seemed to Wiemann that the liner listed rapidly to starboard, while the railings in the dome and various wall fixtures came crashing down onto the first deck and then onto the tables themselves.

He helped a woman up the sharply tilted crowded stairs, calling out all the while:

"Take your time, she's not going down!" But he didn't believe a word of it himself. He thought the entire "inside" of the *Lusitania* must have been blown out by the explosion. He was not frightened, but more curious to get on deck to see what was happening and what he could do there.

Robert Timmins, the cotton man from Texas, never had his second dish of ice cream. What he had heard sounded like a "penetrating thrust," as though the torpedo had pierced all the way through the ship and out the other side.

He and Moodie, also from Texas, immediately pushed their chairs back and noticed the ship sharply listing even before they had cleared the First Class dining saloon. Without feeling any particular sense of haste, they walked down to their cabin on the port side for lifebelts. The list was extremely acute as they groped inside the tumbled litter of their cabin.

The two went up to the starboard side of the boat deck, where they immediately helped two sailors lower a boat with about sixty persons in it.

Close beside Timmins was George Kessler, the New York wine merchant who had brought 2,000,000 dollars in securities with him. Smoking a cigar, he helped to load the boats with women. He told Timmins he was doing so only "in a spirit of convention" as he did not believe the *Lusitania* would sink.

Then Timmins thought he saw, on the bridge at the forward end of the boat deck, the short, stocky figure of Captain Turner, with one hand raised, as a referee would his hand in an athletic contest to stop the play. Simultaneously a steward came from the bridge with orders to stop lowering.

The *Lusitania* still had too much momentum and was

plunging ahead out of control as the green water sloshed past her sides.

As if to punctuate the steward's words, there was a smacking crash against the water, quick screams, then silence. Timmins looked over to see a lifeboat dangling from one of its falls . . . it had been lowered too hastily by one end and its occupants were spilled out before it had quite reached the water.

Timmins watched with a strange, almost stolid objectivity as though this were something detached from his own existence.

Among those who had been in the boat were A. C. Bilicke, fifty-four-year-old builder and real estate man of Los Angeles, Mrs. Bilicke, and the Reverend David Loynd, British-born Baptist minister from Richmond, Indiana, and his wife, Alice.

Timmins continued to stare at the half-smashed boat, the crushed bodies in the water, a few survivors swimming. Then he saw people arriving, presumably from the steerage but in orderly fashion. He felt the ship lean "farther and lower" and knew the situation was becoming worse. A woman from Second Class pleaded with him for a lifebelt. He gave her his.

Next a mother from Third, with her baby and her emaciated husband who seemed to be suffering from tuberculosis, came over to Timmins, drawn to him as though the man's very bulk inspired confidence. He advised her to strap the baby in front of her, with its face to hers, then started to assist her. The sickly husband appeared frightened.

"Do you think they will live, sir?" Timmins recalled him asking.

"I think so," the cotton dealer answered, then added bluntly, "but you won't."

Bestic, who had started for the baggage room, never made it. Within seconds after the explosion word reached him that everyone down there had been lost, including dozens of seamen who were skilled in lifeboat launching and handling. Among other things, the lift had torn loose, trapping those not killed outright by the explosion.

As he came out on deck he was impressed with the "strange silence" that had fallen over the ship, interrupted in those first few moments only by the whimpering of a child, the cry of a sea gull. Then there came a gathering background babble of confusion like a rising wind in a bewitched forest.

Bestic ran out to his boat station, Number 10 on the port side. He supervised the lowering of the lifeboat down to the rail, but because of the increasing list it landed on the deck.

At that point Captain Anderson arrived to study the launching attempt. He had an idea for righting the ship.

"Go to the bridge and tell them they are to trim her with the port [ballast] tanks," he ordered.

Bestic quickly made his way to the bridge and sang out the order to Second Officer Hefford, who repeated it. Then Bestic returned to Number 10 lifeboat.

Launchings all along the port side were attended with the same difficulties as Bestic had with Number 10. Those boats which with herculean efforts, were finally pushed out and over the sides, bumped down and past the two-inch-wide "snap-headed" rivets that protruded almost a full inch above the ship's plates. It became quickly apparent that this would scrape their bottoms off as well as wrench their sternposts loose.

A man, seated in one of the boats and "paralyzed with

fear," compounded the difficulties by ignoring the officer's command to get out. A sailor leaped in with an ax.

"Hop it!" he commanded, with a threatening move of the ax.

The man obeyed promptly.

It became impossible to launch any more boats on this side.

Leith, in his nearby radio shack, kept tapping out the message, monotonously, insistently:

Come at once. Big list. Ten miles south Old Head Kinsale. . . . MSU.

Then the ammeter needle on the transmitter panel wavered, came back, sank to O, stayed there. Leith tapped the glass face. The ship's generators had failed.

He left his chair and quickly switched on the emergency batteries. These were kept charged by a dynamo driven in turn by a small gasoline engine. The sparks danced from his key once more:

Come at once. Big list. Ten miles south Old Head Kinsale.

The clock above the transmitter read 2:14 P.M.

10

The SOS from the *Lusitania* was picked up at once by many radio operators. They all knew the ship and her code letters, and the news was electrifying. They pressed the headsets closer to their ears and strained to catch any further amplification of the stark announcement.

The British tanker *Narragansett*, owned by the Anglo-American Oil Company, bound from Liverpool for Bayonne, New Jersey, was thirty-five miles southeast of the big Cunarder's estimated position when Talbot Smith, her wireless operator, received the distress call.

"*Dit-dit-dit . . . dah-dah-dah . . . dit-dit-dit . . .* SOS" . . . ran the familiar International Morse Code signal for help, now known to everyone since the *Titanic* wrote it in anguish into the language of the sea.

Smith scribbled it on his pad and raced out of his shack and around the corner to the bridge. He handed it to Captain Charles L. Harwood. Harwood's reaction was instantaneous. He altered the course to the northwest, then ordered "Full speed ahead!" He hoped to arrive at the Old Head of Kinsale by dead reckoning.

The 9196-ton *Narragansett* was neither a new ship nor fast. But somehow her engineers pushed her speed up from a bare eleven knots to slightly better than fourteen.

She throbbed and trembled in every rivet and plate, belched black smoke from her stacks, and rolled heavily ahead. It was as if some weary old coaster were suddenly seized with the delusion that it was a destroyer. Old-timers on her decks shook their heads as they eyed the lifebelt lockers.

Yet some remembered that the *Narragansett* was an old hand at rescue. When the passenger liner *Volturno* burned in mid-Atlantic two years before, the *Narragansett* answered her distress call. Particularly needed was a tanker, to pour oil on the stormy seas and enable other ships to transfer the souls from the blazing *Volturno*.

The *Narragansett,* by her own answer, at that time added her bit to the timeless sayings of the sea, as her Marconi man promised:

. . . will come with the milk in the morning!

At almost the same instant that Captain Harwood of the *Narragansett* read the *Lusitania*'s SOS, Captain W. F. Wood of the Leyland Line freighter, *Etonian,* out of Liverpool for Boston, did exactly the same thing. His own "Sparks" had appeared excitedly with a scrawled radio message.

The *Etonian,* grossing 6400 tons, was about seven miles astern of the *Narragansett.* Between the two was a third westbound vessel, the *City of Exeter,* owned by the Ellerman Lines and skippered by Captain G. R. Rae. It was only a year old, and larger than either of the other two. All three had been in radio contact with one another.

Now the *Etonian* and the *City of Exeter* were coaling up and taking the wraps off their own boiler safety valves to follow in the *Narragansett*'s wake. Any sailor knew, when a huge passenger liner was in trouble, that help could not arrive too fast.

The message was also picked up on shore, at the Signal Station on the Old Head of Kinsale itself, at Land's End, England, at Radio Valencia. It was unquestionably heard by the powerful German Admiralty wireless stations, too, at Heligoland, Wilhelmshaven, and Emden.

The signal station at Kinsale immediately passed the message to Rear Admiral Sir Charles Coke, commanding the naval station at Queenstown. His duty officer cranked the telephone next to his desk and called operations office at Deep Water Quay.

The small tugs *Julia, Flying Fish, Warrior,* and *Stormcock* were readied for sea.

Word also reached Rear Admiral H. L. A. Hood, just arrived to take command of the Irish Coast Patrol. He started his men casting off moorings of his flagship, the ancient cruiser *Juno,* and three others in his squadron, the *Isis, Sutlej,* and *Venus.*

Admiral Hood strode across the cramped bridge of the *Juno* and glanced nervously up at the spires of St. Colman's Cathedral rising out of Queenstown, the massive rock emplacements of Spy Hill dominating the background. All of these landmarks should be drawing astern even now, if only his lubberly crew could stop fumbling and hurry!

After his implied reprimand for the state of the Dover patrol, this new situation already looked black. Somehow he felt he was headed for another "failure."

Tenders, fishing craft . . . the *Bluebell* and *Lady Elsie* among them . . . small harbor motorboats, and lifeboats with rowers heard the word in minutes, even though none had wireless sets. All along the south Irish coast, from Bantry Bay to St. George's Channel, seamen learned that the *Lusitania* was in distress. A flotilla of some two dozen assorted craft, of all shapes and sizes, now prepared to answer the SOS.

A group of observers had been gathered for hours on the headland of Kinsale. They had watched the sailing ship *Earl of Latham* sink under a rocketing of shellfire only two days before. They had known there must be at least one submarine in the area and also that the big liner was due sometime today.

John Harrington, a fisherman; John J. Murphy, a fifteen-year-old boy; and L. McCarthy, a coast guardsman, were among those near Kinsale Light on the rough, rugged promontory. Some sat on stone walls which fenced the lighthouse area, and shared space with the pigs and chickens of the lightkeeper.

There were also a number of schoolchildren, excused from classes to be there.

None was disappointed.

They saw the *Lusitania,* with her imposing four-stacked silhouette and wisping smoke, appear around Seven Head's Point, grow into unmistakable size before their vision . . . they saw her alter course . . . and they heard the detonation of the torpedo.

"It was a sort of heavy rumble like a distant foghorn," was the way young Murphy described it.

He and all the others, breathlessly, saw the steam and the

smoke shoot up. They watched the huge ship list and begin to settle.

In the history of Kinsale—extending back several thousand years—never had there been a spectacle like this one.

CHAPTER 11

Quartermaster Hugh Robert Johnston, at the helm, watched the list indicator beneath the compass. It was a small pendulum, showing how far the ship might sway from even keel to either side. It had staggered wildly when the *Lusitania* was hit, then recovered to read a steady starboard list of 15 degrees. The spirit level just above it had bubbled drunkenly. During the ensuing four minutes, however, the little brass indicator fluctuated greatly.

When at first Johnston was able to bring the ship's bow on Kinsale, he felt relief in spite of the hammering of his heart. But when the liner kept swinging to port, with considerable headway on, Johnston suspected the battle was lost.

"Hard a-starboard!" Captain Turner sang out as he paced between the port bridge wing and the helm. He repeated the order, but there was no response. The *Lusitania*'s bow kept tracing an arc toward the infinite blue horizon seaward. The quartermaster, who had responded earlier with a 35-degree change in the rudder, believed now that the steering mechanism had "frozen" in that position—meaning the ship would now continue in her wide, slow arc.

Next Turner ordered the engines reversed to check the vessel. Again there was no response. No doubt remained in Turner's mind that the engines were fully "out of commission."

Turner sent Staff Captain Anderson onto the boat deck to call a temporary halt to the launching of lifeboats. Then he walked over to the binnacle and stared at the list indicator as though, by his gaze, he might somehow alter its disturbing tilt. It is alarming to any mariner to watch his ship lean precariously to one side without recovering and tracing a corresponding roll to the other.

"Keep your eye on her to see if she goes any further," he said to Johnston, then ordered Second Officer Hefford below to the forecastle head to close watertight doors. Before he left, Hefford also warned Johnston:

"Keep your eye on the indicator on the compass and the spirit level and sing out if she goes any further!"

Their orders were quite redundant as far as the veteran quartermaster was concerned, for he shared their dread of the *Lusitania*'s capsizing.

The indicator continued to hang at a fairly constant 15 degrees, and there did seem a chance that the *Lusitania* would go no further. Johnston recalled several improperly loaded or ballasted freighters he had served on which had listed this much all the way across the Atlantic. Unbalanced shoveling from port and starboard coal bunkers could have the same result.

There was another faint gleam of hope: it seemed as though she were coming closer to land all the time. The hills of Ireland were etched sharply, and somewhere between them and the liner was a "black speck" that appeared to be a fishing smack.

If she could last for just an hour, Turner might succeed in beaching the ship. Of one thing Johnston, like others of the crew, was confident: he was sailing under as brave a captain as ever walked a navigation bridge.

Then the indicator moved again: 16, 17, 18, 19 . . . finally 20 degrees list to starboard. Johnston watched. It showed no tendency to recover.

At that moment Chief Officer Piper called out to Captain Turner:

"I'm going down to the fo'csle to help Hefford with the hatches—she seems to be sinking fast by the bow! Perhaps we can slow her a bit!"

He raced away from the bridge.

"T-w-e-n-t-y degrees to starboard!" Johnston sung out in a loud clear voice to Turner, who was now the only other person near the wheelhouse. The whole bridge seemed suddenly deserted.

Johnston felt useless at the helm. He feared, as he watched the indicator, that it would not stop swinging until the *Lusitania* had turned all the way over onto her side. The thought filled him with a cold and hopeless terror.

Far below, Senior Second Engineer Cockburn and Senior Third Little surveyed the chaos in their once orderly world of machinery. The gong that sounded shoveling instructions was silenced. In Number 1 stokehold Thomas Madden stood undecided in front of the center boiler. He was sweating furiously.

Those who remained of the "black gang" of stokers were deafened from the concussion. The nightmare of war had happened. Five pounds a month was little enough wages to stew in an inferno of more than 100 degrees, but this . . .

Stoker Madden figured the detonation had come from the

forward side of the starboard boiler. Now water was cascading into his boiler room as though one of the innumerable bulkheads had given way under the weight of sea water in the starboard side.

He knew the turbines had stopped. Astern of him, and on a slightly higher level, they usually added their roar to the reassuring pulse of the four spinning propeller shafts. Now he heard only the menacing sound of escaping steam.

To be burned or drowned was bad enough but, somehow, being scalded to death seemed worse. The water—green, dark, and greasy—surged over Madden's feet. It felt like ice to his overheated legs. He looked at the hot coals in the furnace in front of him and the water pouring on to them; the steam would be scalding.

Madden threw down his shovel and ran to the watertight door. It was securely shut. He banged on it until his knuckles stung, then realized the futility of it and rushed back to his station in front of the center boiler. He saw sea water "coming through the boilers." He estimated it to be about a foot and a half deep over the floor grating.

Madden started toward the escape ladder, one of several narrow-runged ladders which pinpointed up through air shafts to glass-covered hatches on the boat deck. The force of the incoming sea knocked him over. For a moment he was completely submerged in the cold, dirty water. It tasted briny and he sat up blind and coughing.

The lights had flickered out and he was in the dark except for the glow from the furnaces. He stood up, heavy from the water, and struggled toward the ladder in the ventilator.

Several decks above Madden, and astern, Martin Mannion, of St. Louis, was also in trouble. His companions, who had been playing poker with him in Second Class smoking saloon for most of the voyage, had deserted him within seconds after the torpedo hit. When he looked about the room, tilted at a crazy angle, he saw all the other tables were empty, too, many chairs upturned.

There was just one more possibility—the bartender. Mannion made his way "uphill" to the bar.

"Let's die game anyway," he proposed to the bartender.

The bartender eyed Mannion from two red, bulging eyes even as he untied his apron.

"You go to hell!" he cried, clearing the counter with one leap. He bolted through the littered smoking saloon and toward the door leading on deck.

Mannion shrugged and clambered with some difficulty over the bar. From the splintered heap of broken glass he salvaged a bottle of ale and opened it.

On the boat deck, Lady Mackworth watched fascinated as passengers streamed up from Third Class. They seemed to be fighting their way into a boat near her. They looked white-faced and "terrified," and there was no kind of order, in her estimation, as the strong pushed the weaker aside. She was struck by the apparent absence of discipline.

Here and there a man had his arm around a woman's waist and bore her along. But there were no children to be seen. She believed that children could not have survived in the pushing, "shrieking" throng.

"I always thought a shipwreck was a well-organized affair," she said to Dorothy Connor.

"So did I," Dorothy agreed, "but I've learnt a devil of a lot in the last five minutes."

Farther along the deck, Isaac Lehmann, New York export broker, was attempting his own method of organization. He had gone to his cabin for his revolver and was waving it, not at the Third Class passengers, but at the crewmen. At the command relayed by Staff Captain Anderson, they had paused in launching a boat.

"I'll shoot the first man who refuses to assist in launching!" Lehmann shouted to the dumfounded crewmen, then punctuated his threat: "To hell with the Captain!"

The sailors obeyed and freed the boat from its chocks, while some passengers were climbing into it. But, with all Lehmann's desire to speed up lifesaving, the launching did not turn out quite as he had hoped. The boat swung prematurely out, dumping its occupants into the sea.

Other boats were also being lowered in contradiction to orders from the bridge. The crewmen seemed torn between instinctive obedience and the dictates of their own immediate judgment.

One boat tilted until it was almost perpendicular and tossed out half its occupants. It did not capsize, however, and the remaining occupants scrambled back aboard.

Now Lady Mackworth, who had seen the incident, turned away. She decided it was "not safe to look at horrible things." At the same time she was struck by the fact that no one in her little group was making any attempt to board a boat. Some voiced fears that the submarine would machine-gun them once in the water.

She noticed a number of people moving about the deck, "gently and vaguely" like "a swarm of bees who do not know where the queen has gone."

Dr. Fisher, who had been standing like an observer at a football game, decided to go below for lifebelts. No sooner had he left than word was passed that the bulkheads had been closed and the danger was over. As if in confirmation, the *Lusitania* measurably righted herself.

For a brief moment the group felt relieved.

Then there was an ominous creaking in the liner's plates, beams, and joints as she rolled over again, this time even further, onto her beam. Chairs and tables, crockery, anything not bolted down, made a frightening clatter inside.

Theodate Pope and Edwin Friend were "sickened" too by the sight of the up-ended lifeboat. They continued past Lady Mackworth and Dorothy Connor down to B Deck on the starboard side where they watched another boat being lowered safely past the deck and on into the water. It occurred to her and Friend that the ship was sinking quickly, that if it did plunge under it would fall over onto the lifeboats and capsize them.

"It's not a good place to jump from," Theodate said.

They turned to make their way through the crush of people on B Deck and to the ladder on which they had just descended from the boat deck. They walked close together side by side, arms about each other's waists.

Before reaching the steep stairway they encountered Mme de Page. On one side of her was Dr. Houghton. A man not known to Theodate was on the other. The Belgian woman had been busily calming children, a few women as well, and assisting them into lifeboats. She had just finished bandaging the hand of a man who had hurt himself while helping the crew lower the boats: Matt Freeman, amateur lightweight boxing champion of England.

Now Dr. Houghton fastened Marie de Page's lifebelt securely about her and advised her to be prepared to jump. Theodate thought the Belgian woman's eyes were "wide and startled, but brave." The Connecticut woman started to greet her, then realized it was no time for words unless "one could offer help." The pair gained the upper deck and watched several more boats being safely lowered.

"You better get in," Friend told her, pointing to a rapidly filling boat.

A chance acquaintance of Friend's, Ernest Cowper, the newspaperman, was helping a six-year-old girl named Helen Smith into the same boat. Elizabeth Hampshire, from Derbyshire, England, took her on her lap.

"She asked me to save her," Cowper explained with a trace of smile. "Says she can't find her mother and father or baby sister Bessie, but her grandparents'll be waiting in Liverpool."

Theodate, like Lady Mackworth, was appalled at the lack of children in lifeboats, and wondered if something had happened in the nursery, or whether the absence of boat drills and now the general lack of organization had made it impossible for the little ones to know what to do or where to go.

She found herself speculating about mothers like Mrs. Hodges who had said, "If we go down, we'll all go down together," or like Mrs. Crompton and her six children, who sat up forward in the dining saloon. She had not seen either family since the torpedo hit.

Theodate refused to enter a boat without Friend and he in turn would not set foot in one so long as women remained on deck. They started "uphill" for the stern as they observed the bow to be sinking. Water was already pouring over it and cascading down the fo'csle ladders into the crew's quarters, the locker room for the huge anchor chains, and other forward storage areas.

Her maid, Emily Robinson, appeared in front of them, and Theodate put a hand on her shoulder. All she could say was, "Oh, Robinson . . ."

Robinson's "habitual smile" was frozen on her face. Even Theodate, worldly and circumspect as she thought herself, was transfixed by that look.

"Lifebelts!" Friend snapped, rousing his companion from her temporary trance. The two ducked into the nearest suites, which now were in a completely disordered state, and found three "Boddy's Patent" belts.

Robert Wiemann had just made his way up to the promenade deck. It seemed to him people were running as best they could toward the stern. The waiter rushed along with them. This was the part of the ship in which Wiemann lived, and he knew there were lifebelts in a locker at the foot of the stairs to his cabin!

The stairs ran from port to starboard. Though it was nearly perpendicular now, Wiemann managed to get down by holding the rail. Others crawled on hands and knees. Wiemann had just grabbed three or four belts when the ship gave a threatening lurch.

He fastened one belt on a woman and one on himself. The others he dropped on the deck as he helped pass the women and children up to the boat deck.

James Brooks did not risk going inside to fetch lifebelts. He continued around the decks. About the first time around, as he passed beneath the bridge, he saw Captain Turner hold up his hands and order:

"Lower no more boats! Everything is going to be all right!"

Brooks kept on, becoming more calm as he walked. It was then he saw the first boat spill its occupants into the sea.

If only they could slow the *Lusitania,* he thought, long enough to get the boats safely into the water. It did seem, however, that—out of control or not—the liner was plunging

On the morning of May 1, 1915, this Cunard ad appeared in New York newspapers. To its left is the warning inserted by the Imperial German Embassy.

Here is the *Lusitania*, once queen of the Cunard fleet: 790 feet long, weighing 32,000 tons, she could cross the Atlantic in 4½ days. (*Imperial War Museum Photo*)

These passengers are on the boat deck. They may have been nurses who were en route to La Panne. *(Photo courtesy Brown Brothers)*

The skyline of Manhattan was seen by passengers on the port side of the boat deck as the *Lusitania* left New York. *(Photo courtesy Brown Brothers)*

Elbert Hubbard, the sage of East Aurora, was Europe-bound to meet the Kaiser. *(International News Photo)*

A confident captain, William Thomas Turner, smiles on the bridge of his ship. *(Photo courtesy Brown Brothers)*

Charles Frohman, greatest producer of his time, was off to Europe on his annual trip. His protégés there included Barrie, Pinero, and Maugham. *(Photo courtesy Underwood & Underwood)*

Alfred Gwynne Vanderbilt, multimillionaire and sports enthusiast, was off to England for a horse show. Both he and Frohman were lost. *(Photo courtesy Underwood & Underwood)*

The luxurious saloons like the one pictured above were a feature of the *Lusitania*. This one was occupied by socializing passengers when the torpedo struck. (*Photo courtesy Brown Brothers*)

In the engine room, pictured at right, the torpedo took a heavy toll of the *Lusitania's* crew. The man at the gears bears a striking resemblance to chief engineer Archibald Bryce. (*Photo courtesy Brown Brothers*)

On Saturday, May 8, news of the sinking the day before made front pages everywhere. In New York *The World* claimed erroneously that the submarine had used two torpedoes to sink the great liner.

This mysterious scrap of paper was found in a bottle buried in the sand of an English beach long after the torpedoing. Its origin has never been traced. *(National Archives Photo)*

Anxious crowds sought news of the *Lusitania's* survivors from the Cunard office in Liverpool. When this street filled, other crowds formed and surged around the city. (*National Archives Photo*)

Among the survivors were these two thankful women, shown as they arrived at Euston Station, London, several days after the sinking. *(Mirrorpic Photo)*

This group of survivors was pitifully clad in borrowed or salvaged clothing. The meager bundles they carry probably represent all that remains of their possessions. *(National Archives Photo)*

Ellen Smith, 6, of Ellwood City, Pa., clutches her doll, all she had left. She had lost her mother, father, and little sister Bessie—and owed her own life to Ernest Cowper, Toronto newspaperman. *(National Archives Photo)*

Shock and exposure affected many of the survivors. These two, who had been in the water for hours, found little to smile about. *(Mirrorpic Photo)*

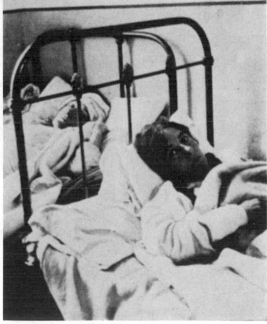

The survivor on the right is wearing a British officer's great-coat. His possessions were lost when the ship went down. (*National Archives Photo*)

Lieutenant Hugh Allan talks with a survivor outside the Cunard office in Liverpool. His mother, Lady Allan, survived, but his twin sisters, Gwen and Anna, were lost. *(National Archives Photo)*

Without a command, wearing his shrunken uniform and makeshift cap, Captain Turner walks uncertainly through Queenstown. He had thought he was the last person to leave the ship. *(National Archives Photo)*

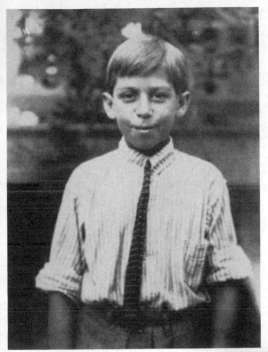

Edward Williams, 10, . . .

. . . and his sister . . . Edith, 12, were saved, but their mother and her four other children were drowned when the ship went down. (*National Archives Photo*)

On Monday, May 10, all of Ireland mourned as the first group of more than one hundred victims of the *Lusitania* were laid to rest in common graves. *(National Archives Photo)*

toward the Old Head of Kinsale on a remarkably straight course.

Then a crewman, wearing a double-breasted seaman's jacket, passed Brooks on deck swinging a revolver in his hand. The Bridgeport chains representative heard him say that no one could get in the boats. Brooks replied, "Who in hell is trying to?"

In the next instant he recognized Staff Captain Anderson, coatless, running toward the stern. But Jay Brooks did not have long to speculate just where he was going or why he was in such a hurry, for he glimpsed at least sixty women hanging onto the iron pipe railing, apparently unable or afraid to let go and lower themselves into a lifeboat.

"Come on, ladies, I'll help you," he called. Tall and husky, he inspired immediate confidence. Holding onto the boat davit with one arm, Brooks grabbed the women one by one as they jumped from the boat deck to the lifeboat. Only a strong person could have done it.

Florence Padley emerged from the stair onto the boat deck to hear the staff captain calling:

"It's all right. We're making for the shore."

Land did not seem that reassuringly close to her, but neither did the chances of getting away in a lifeboat, though she saw others leaving the ship safely. Finally she saw one boat with only a few people in it, and started toward it.

When the torpedo struck, Professor Holbourn had thought of lifebelts at once. Finding none on deck, he took his twelve-year-old friend Avis Dolphin to his cabin corridor. Little Avis was feeling somewhat like Dorothy in the new *Oz* book, whose familiar and secure world had been sent topsy-turvy by a cyclone.

The professor's cabin was a mess. Such articles as his toothbrush, razor, and lotions rolled about the floor. Wide-open wardrobe doors revealed suits that hung crazily out into the room. His broad-brimmed black hat had sailed off the closet shelf and lodged itself in the corner behind the door.

Worst of all, the porthole was no longer reassuringly divided, like a well-sliced pie, into equal parts of sea and sky. It was all bright blue, motionless.

Holbourn had to pull himself up the sloping deck by grabbing first at the bed, then the wardrobe door, to which he clung with one hand as he groped on the shelf for the belts. He was afraid the wardrobe would topple over on him.

Finally he skidded back into the corridor and fastened a belt on Avis. Carrying two extras back to the deck, he and Avis met her traveling companions. One, Miss Smith, refused Holbourn's offer of a belt, reminding him that he had a wife and three children dependent on him. So he tied it on himself, under protest, as the group went in search of a boat.

Holbourn put Avis in a lifeboat as it was being swung out, then was momentarily distracted by the sight of two men, stripped naked, diving off the boat deck. They struck out toward a boat that was floating, smashed, on the water. Holbourn was amazed to see how quickly the pair were swept astern, and he deduced that the *Lusitania* was still traveling at a considerable speed.

He continued around the decks, offering lifebelts to some of Avis' friends and helping them into boats. Since he was a champion swimmer himself, he resolved he would go forward and swim for it, without trusting to the boats or the way some were being lowered.

By now Herbert Ehrhardt had reunited the girl's brother with his family. He realized from the difficulty of walking that the list was increasing more and more rapidly and that the *Lusitania* would sink before all the lifeboats were launched. It was then he "became frightened."

When the deck began to slope, he had to sit to prevent himself from losing his balance. Others were sliding down the deck all the way to the railings. Ehrhardt became still more alarmed and wondered whether he would be able to avoid bumping into people and hurting them if he slipped. As he noticed the bow awash, which caused a "tremendous turmoil in the water" it occurred to him that it might really be impossible for anyone to swim in the vortex.

This "turmoil" in the seas and the growing litter of deck chairs, empty lifeboats, and other menacing debris being tossed about, made him realize that he might be experiencing his last few seconds of life. He began to roll himself over as he slipped down the deck, hoping thus to avoid bumping anyone below him and wondering whether he would hit the rails or the water first. He remembered saying to himself:

"I'm better off than most of these as I've nobody dependent on me."

And then he started a silent, personal prayer for his fiancée and his mother.

Archie Donald was watching a fireman who poised momentarily on the rail before taking an almost professional dive into the water. Its grace, to Donald, seemed to have no fitting place in this holocaust.

Then he heard the sound of a boat running through davits and looked in time to see it smash to pieces in the water. He figured that the ropes must have been too short. He saw several people bobbing around in the water.

The fireman who had taken the beautiful dive swam until he reached the stern of the ship, then disappeared from view. Inspired by the fireman's performance, Donald decided that the "best policy" was to leave the ship, fast. When he saw an empty beer box with two handles, it occurred to him that here was a made-to-order life preserver.

First he deliberately removed his wrist watch so it would not get wet. Then, taking his pocket watch from his coat, he carefully placed both in his left-hand trouser pocket. Next he stripped off his coat.

Holding the beer case with a fierce grip, Donald started to climb the stairs to the next deck. He encountered Dr. R. J. R. Mecredy, of Dublin, whom he knew slightly, coming hand over hand down the outside of the companionway. The young Irish physician was wearing a lifebelt and carrying another in his hand.

"Where did you get the lifebelts?" Archie Donald asked, almost in surprise.

"Down in the cabins," Dr. Mecredy answered, explaining that he had first queued up before a deck storage locker, but the supply of lifebelts had run out. He reported also that the water had been pouring through the porthole in his cabin.

Archie had not thought about belts, but luckily discovered he was on the port side of the same deck on which his cabin was situated. He noticed that a door, battened the entire voyage, had been opened. He ran through it and down the lightless passage and into his cabin. The list was so bad that he found walking extremely difficult.

He felt around in the locker and on one side of the dark cabin, and realized the belts were missing. They were gone from the other side too. He groped through the litter of the cabin that had been his home for six days until he finally found one last remaining belt. It occurred to him that if the list became worse, he might soon be walking on the walls—a thought shocking to his sense of proportion.

Archie left his cabin and continued on the port side up to the boat deck. There he saw a sight going virtually unnoticed by the other passengers. Norman Stone, of Vancouver, a veteran of General Pershing's expedition after Pancho Villa on the Mexican border, was methodically tearing all the clothing from his wife.

In the brilliant sunshine, and with the privacy of Times Square, Stone did not desist until Mrs. Stone, unprotesting, was stripped down to her stockings. Then he fastened her lifebelt securely around her, lessening to some degree her nakedness.

Donald, preoccupied as the others with his own salvation, was impressed simply with the fact that Stone "seemed to know exactly what to do." Now Stone started ripping the canvas off a nearby collapsible boat, something which the men thought should have been done long before. Archie helped him.

As he was on the port side, he noticed how terribly high the deck was above the water. He watched some people get into a lifeboat, heard its bumping-scraping descent over the plates and rivets of the sloping side. He didn't see how it could ever reach the water intact.

Archie wondered why he was not frightened. His thoughts came with a clarity that surprised him.

He decided to cross "downhill" to the First Class portion. There, he helped load a boat, fending off a group of grimy, frantic stokers who were crowding toward it.

"The women must be put in first!" he shouted. Other men joined with him in keeping the "black gang" off.

Finally, when about twenty women were in the boat, the men standing on the deck of the *Lusitania* began to lower away. This boat was lowered too fast by the forward fall, while the aft one seemed to stick in the block. Someone cut the ropes which were retarding the operation, but it was too late. Everyone had been dumped into the sea.

Donald watched the boat's passengers struggle onto a rope netting attached to a lower deck, and climb higher as the water reached them. He recognized one of them—May Bird, a stewardess. It seemed strange to see her hair streaming all over her face, her usually starched uniform clinging soddenly like wet laundry.

As he shifted his gaze back to those still on deck, he noticed Elbert Hubbard and his wife Alice. Although he had never met them, he knew at once who they were. They looked "very gray-haired" and were holding hands. He heard them refuse to be helped into a boat.

It was the same Elbert Hubbard who, in his writings, had philosophized, "We are here now, some day we shall go. And when we go we would like to go gracefully."

Nearby was Timmins, from Texas, surrounded by a group of steerage passengers, a number of whom seemed to be Russians. While Timmins could not recognize their gabbling, he was trying to reassure them. He held up a hand, nodded his head and repeated:

"All right, all right!"

They appeared to understand. One kissed his hand. He forgot what was happening to the ship in his momentary amazement at having his hand kissed.

Timmins, like Lady Mackworth, had heard the order to empty the boats, and the assurances the ship was "safe." He did not share the optimism, although he also noticed the *Lusitania* right herself. His friend Moodie, beside him, asked:

"How about it, old man?"

Timmins shook his head. He believed the liner was even then "gone." He figured the water had surged over her longitudinal bulkheads, which would indicate that ocean was pouring in at a terrific rate. He decided against communicating his gloomy conclusions to the steerage passengers.

All the way aft on the promenade deck, Able Seaman Thomas Mahoney, who had spotted a "suspicious" object about half an hour before, was trying to help six terrified men and women down from a curious refuge. They were all perched on the awning above the veranda café, struggling to climb to the deck below.

"Get on my shoulders!" he instructed them. His height made this a very probable solution to their dilemma.

But while they were trying to obey, the awning spars broke and all six fell in a heap on top of him.

Close by, oblivious to all else, a frightened passenger, Mrs. Stewart Mason, was seeking help.

"Where's my husband?" wailed the dark-haired young bride from Boston. The tears welled in her eyes.

Oliver P. Bernard was doing his best to comfort her.

"It's all right now, we go ashore directly, so don't worry," he said.

Leslie Mason kept staring at Bernard "like one demented," as she asked, "Where's my husband?" Bernard had known her father, William Lindsey, in Boston. Now he took the girl by the shoulders and shook her.

"Stay right here," he said. "Don't move from this spot and your husband will find you here, surely, as they will be lowering the boats from this side. I'll find some lifebelts in case we need them." He told her to pull herself together.

With something to do, Bernard acquired a determination that salved his own fears. As he hurried below he kept thinking of the torpedo wake streaking toward the *Lusitania,* striking it with "a slight shock as if a tug had run into the enormous hull." He had been especially concerned about the glass roofs of the dining saloon, the lounge and veranda café —the splinters could be as deadly as shrapnel.

As he was about to enter First Class quarters through one of the saloon doors, Bernard almost ran into Alfred Gwynne Vanderbilt. Bareheaded, dressed in a dark pinstripe suit, he was holding what looked like a lady's large jewel case. Vanderbilt appeared to the scenic artist as though he were waiting "for the next race at Ascot."

He grinned at Bernard "as if amused by the excitement." Bernard had been thinking about the multimillionaire just before the torpedo struck—"a man with nothing better to do than drive a four-in-hand to Brighton and come three thousand miles to do it."

America, Bernard believed, was "lousy with idle rich." He disliked the very wealthy with an intensity more deeply rooted than a mere distaste for their money, ostentation, yachts and "homes like royal brothels."

The strange spectacle of existence often preyed on the thoughtful artist's mind. This morning, considering himself in the third person as was his custom, he put it this way, "If only he could believe in God, if he could only believe in life as eternal, instead of nursing a despairing conviction that life was not really worth living, that the end of all life lay in the dust, with men and women, dogs and fleas sharing the same fate as blades of grass—flourishing for a moment and then trodden into oblivion."

Bernard could not forget Vanderbilt's grin. He himself was not amused as he ran downstairs to B Deck. Preoccupied, he forgot to allow for the list. He crashed "painfully" at the bottom of the stairs, then picked himself up and limped on.

All lights were out, the passage smoky and in darkness. It was deserted. He fell several times. Once he rolled down a side passage for a few feet before he could stop. Somehow he arrived at the Masons' cabin and called:

"Stewart!"

There was no answer from the darkened, littered state-room and so he went on. He located his own cabin readily because it was at the extreme end of the passage. He knew his lifebelt was stowed on top of the wardrobe. As he felt for it, the heavy cabinet leaned over, and he had the momentary horror that he would drown "like a rat" in the darkness.

He climbed on the berth and worked from the side of the wardrobe, finally dragging his lifebelt out. There were stairs at this end of the passage which he used to return to deck, wondering why he had not thought of them before. He found Leslie Mason had gone.

A woman spied him holding his lifebelt and screamed, "Where did you get that, where did you get it?"

He allowed her to snatch it, then continued around the decks to see what had become of the Masons. Many boats had already gone, but the deck remained crowded with people "frantic" to follow.

A stoker reeled by "as if drunk." His face was a scarlet smear and the crown of his head had been opened up like a "spongy bloody pudding." It made Bernard wonder how many others had been maimed or killed outright by the explosion. He thought of the nursery, the women in their cabins with babies they could not leave.

Now it occurred to Bernard there might not be enough boats for everyone, nor was he sure he wanted to leave on a lifeboat, considering the way some of them were handled.

He'd seen at least one dump its human cargo into the water. In one of them was a girl whom a young man had persuaded to step into it.

Bernard climbed above the boat deck and onto the more narrow Marconi deck. From there he could look down upon the terrifying spectacle with almost Olympian detachment.

The strains of the "Blue Danube," which he had heard at lunch, throbbed in his brain. And he could still smell the distinctive "foody" aroma from the dining saloon. But the only question in his mind was how soon would the *Lusitania* sink?

Some distance out he spied a man swimming on his back. He was naked and paddling gently, smiling up at the ship. And that started Bernard thinking. He stood up and removed some of his clothes, first his coat, vest, collar, and necktie. He put his tiepin in his trouser pocket and then folded the clothes neatly and placed them at the base of the broad, towering funnel. It occurred to him that this following of habit was now preposterous.

With a half-weary resignation, he thought of the futility of life. He seemed to be engulfed in an "awful sadness" and thought that no matter "what fuss he'd made about life," the whole existence amounted to just nothing. His struggles and "petty attainments" were trifles which would be quickly wiped out.

He sighed and started to untie his boots.

In one tiny segment of the spectacle Bernard was watching stood Elizabeth Duckworth. Elizabeth was having trouble finding a boat, as well as maintaining her balance. Fleetingly she thought of all her meager possessions tucked in big, bulging straw suitcases, and despaired of ever seeing them again.

The mate who had picked her up after she stumbled now

helped her into another lifeboat. Someone yelled as she stepped on the person's leg. The rollers wouldn't work and the sailors seemed to be having so much trouble launching it that Elizabeth gathered up her skirts and stepped out onto the sloping deck again. Mrs. Alice Scott, little Arthur's mother, was in this boat.

It was finally launched, while the weaver from Taftville stood on the deck. It went over, spewing its people into the water and against the sides of the ship, which kept plowing ahead as though it never would stop.

Elizabeth watched, horrified as Alice Scott disappeared beneath the churning green waters, heard the others cry out in terror. Alice never came up.

Now Elizabeth started to pray under her breath, "The Lord is my shepherd, therefore can I lack nothing. He shall feed me in a green pasture, and lead me beside the waters of comfort. He shall convert my soul and bring me forth in the paths of righteousness for his Name's sake. Yea, though I walk through the valley of the shadow of death, I will fear no evil . . ."

Next to her three Irish girls were singing, "There Is a Green Hill Not Far Away." They had been humming it gaily before the torpedo struck. Now they sang in cold, choking fright.

In the radio shack Marconi Operator Leith, sweating, too busy to loosen his collar, kept tapping his mariner's requiem:

Come at once. Big list. Ten miles south Old Head Kinsale.

He had to hold onto his table and the transmitter panel to steady himself against the increasing list. He prayed that his message was being received.

Above him the clock read 2:20 P.M.

CHAPTER 12

Charles Lauriat returned on deck wearing one lifebelt, carrying others over his arm. He went directly to the
port side where he had left the Hubbards. They were gone.

He walked aft, offering his belts to those who needed them.
Amazed to note that "about everyone" wore his or her lifebelt incorrectly, he busied himself readjusting them. He kept
on the port side, the high one.

Lauriat paused in his work with the lifebelts long enough
to walk forward again to where he had last seen the Fra and
Alice. He went back more than a dozen times, in utter disbelief that the couple could have vanished so completely.
He stopped Mrs. Padley, who said she had seen the Hubbards standing under a funnel.

Once a woman beside him called toward the bridge:

"Captain, what do you wish us to do?"

"Stay right where you are, Madam, she's all right," the
Boston bookseller heard Captain Turner answer.

"Where do you get your information?" she persisted.

"From the engine room, Madam," Turner said. To Lauriat
he sounded "severe and commanding."

The woman started aft and Lauriat fell in step with her. They tried to reassure the passengers, even though he was certain the liner's end could be measured in minutes. An Italian family, comprised of a grandmother, mother, and three children, "beseeched," him in their own tongue, for aid.

Lauriat returned to his cabin for a few personal possessions that he wanted with him even if he was to perish. This time he descended the same forward companionway Bernard had used, because the main companionway was crowded with people pushing upward.

He groped his way to his cabin through the dark, tilted passageways. By the flickering light of a match he searched quickly through the jumble while the *Lusitania* groaned and rumbled ominously then swayed over still farther.

With his passport and other papers stuffed in his pockets, he left his stateroom and moved back through the passage; one foot on the bulkhead, one on the deck. As he glanced down access passageways which ended with portholes, he saw that the portholes were open. The water could not have been more than a few feet below them. He wondered why these ports had not been closed. He continued on.

When he passed the First Class lounge he noticed that the chairs had fallen over. A few were upturned, with legs straight in the air like dead, rigid horses. The painting over the marble-mantled fireplace hung askew, while the velvet window drapes hung halfway out into the lounge like starched collars strangely out of shape.

On deck, he spied a boat, filled with women and children, hanging securely to its davits. If it were not freed at once, the *Lusitania* would drag it down with her if she sank.

Lauriat jumped into the stern, then realized it was already afloat—the water was flush with the rail of B Deck! The sink-

ing had gained that much momentum in the last few minutes. He freed one end, as a steward at the other hacked
futilely at the thick ropes with a pocket knife.

Lauriat started forward but could make no progress over
the obstructing maze of oars, boat hooks, kegs of water, "and
God knows what."

As the *Lusitania* continued to tilt farther, her funnels
overhung the lifeboat with increasing menace. The people
looked up at the four monstrous black and red specters, and
blanched anew in terror. Some covered their eyes. Lauriat,
caught by the swinging aft davit, was knocked into the
sprawling, clawing mass of people in the bottom of the boat.
He could feel a chill of panic as he struggled to an upright
position and advised the others to jump for it.

"It's your only chance!"

Lauriat went into the 50-degree waters of the Atlantic,
pushing several people ahead of him. In the water he urged
them to put their hands on each others' shoulders to keep in
a group. When he had swum about a hundred feet from the
ship he blinked the cold salt water from his eyes and looked
back.

The decks of the big Cunarder were still filled with people, bunched together and hanging onto stationery objects
to keep their balance. As the water inched up they released
their holds and clawed for upper parts of stanchions.

Many clung to the forlorn hope that they still should stay
with the ship. The Charles A. Plamondons were of this desperate turn of mind. Edward Skay, a steward, spied them together on the promenade deck, refusing his entreaties to try
for a lifeboat.

One lady told Olive North that she thought she would go

into her cabin and at least meet her fate in comfort. She urged Olive to keep her company.

"No, I will make a fight for my life," the English girl replied.

Olive encountered another woman cheerily packing and rearranging her suitcase in magnificent unconcern, as though the ship were now at the very mouth of the Mersey River, approaching Liverpool.

James Brooks helped all sixty of his adopted lady charges into their boat. But the *Lusitania* was listing farther as her decks became almost flush with the surface of the sea. It was hard to free the lifeboats, not from their rope falls and blocks, but from the chains which secured them to the davits. The difficulty was in loosening the clamps which disconnected the chains.

Before the boat with the sixty women could be launched, the boat's keel was afloat. The nearing waters pushed the lifeboat against the davits with a sickening crunch of wood. Most of the women were spilled into the sea.

Brooks knew it was time to go overboard. He had been watching the gathering scum of wooden debris which now was surfacing the sea for hundreds of square yards around the ship. He had no idea where it had all come from or how it had littered the water so quickly. But it made him think of the log-filled Androscoggin at home where, even before he knew much about swimming, he kept himself afloat by hanging onto timbers.

Without bothering to remove his shoes, he jumped into the sea. It did not feel any colder than the Androscoggin; in fact he thought it was "mild."

On the ship, Dr. Mecredy was patiently awaiting his chance for a line down which people were sliding directly into the water. They were making neat, regular little splashes. It seemed a climax consistent with what he considered a disorganized abandoning of the ship, where from the time of torpedoing "everything was quite chaotic."

His descent did not serve to better his opinion. It turned out that the rope was the log line (trailed out astern for recording the ship's run) and made of wire after the first six feet. It was a "very uncomfortable getaway" and he lost considerable skin from his fingers by the time he was in the water. With salt stinging the raw flesh, he struck out for a boat, overloaded though it appeared.

Not far away, the *U-20* was hushed in a silence almost sepulchral, except for the muffled whirr of electric motors. Kapitanleutnant Schwieger was noting in his log:

> She has the appearance of being about to capsize.
> Great confusion on board, boats being cleared and some of them lowered to the water. They must have lost their heads. Many boats crowded come down bow first or stern first in the water and immediately fill and sink. Fewer lifeboats can be made clear owing to the slant of the boat [the *Lusitania*]. The ship blows off, in front appears the name *Lusitania* in gold letters. The stacks were painted black, no stern flag was up. She was running at a speed of twenty sea miles . . .

On the ship the remaining male passengers were making desperate, last-minute attempts to round up the children. They had seen a number being put in lifeboats, but feared many more were trapped below decks.

Father Basil Maturin, "pale but calm," administered absolutions to several people, then was seen handing a child into a lifeboat.

Lindon W. Bates, New York political leader crossing in connection with Belgian relief, kept dashing inside the tilting

black passageways until the water rose to deck level and he
could no longer go below. Then he grabbed a chair for a life
preserver and ran astern. He had already seen two from his
group, Marie de Page and Dr. Houghton, jump into the
water. They had held on to one another.

Commander Stackhouse, explorer and organizer of the
great forthcoming Antarctic expedition aboard the ship *Dis-
covery*, was on deck with Lieutenant Frederick Lasseter, of
the "King's Own Light Infantry." Stackhouse told the
younger man to look for his mother.

When both Lasseters returned, wearing lifebelts, they saw
Stackhouse fasten his own belt on a little girl.

"You better jump," Stackhouse advised. Lasseter, wounded
in the September fighting in Flanders, decided to follow the
advice. He took one last look at Stackhouse assisting women
into a boat, and heard him explaining why he could not join
them: "There are others who must go first."

The Lasseters jumped.

Second Steward Robert Chisholm passed Vanderbilt on B
Deck "vainly attempting to rescue a hysterical woman."

"Hurry Mr. Vanderbilt, or it will be too late!" Chisholm
shouted.

Vanderbilt did not heed the steward. As a matter-of-fact,
one skill in particular had never been mastered by this otherwise athletic young man—he couldn't swim a stroke.

A twenty-five-year-old baby's nurse from Seattle, Alice Middleton, thought she recognized Vanderbilt as her benefactor
as she accepted an offer of a lifebelt. He helped her put it on.

Others heard him telling Ronald Denyer, his valet: "Find
all the kiddies you can, boy!"

Not far away on the same deck, Charles Frohman, a cigar
in his mouth, was a study in calm to the trio around him.

The trio included his pretty actress friend, Rita Jolivet, her brother-in-law, George Vernon and Captain A. J. Scott, an English soldier en route from India via the United States.

"Stay where you are," he had advised. "This is going to be a close call. We shall have more chance here than by rushing for the boats."

They stood arm-in-arm. Finally, forcing Frohman to put on a lifebelt, Scott unfastened his own lifebelt saying, "If you must die, it is only for once."

The producer seemed concerned primarily for the safety of the young actress. He kept looking at her and at one point warned:

"You had better hold onto the rail and save your strength." In a few moments he removed the belt the English soldier had given him and made him assist a hysterical woman into it. As the water rose closer, Frohman remarked with a smile,

" 'Why fear death? It is the most beautiful adventure in life.' "

Rita recognized the quote from *Peter Pan,* by C.F.'s friend and favorite author, James Barrie. But this was no stage set. She knew they were going to have to swim for it, and started to draw her skirts higher about her. Then fear seized her as she realized that Frohman could never survive the cold waters. She stood there, clutching the rail, as the water came up.

Others, like Archie Donald, young and unimpeded by rheumatism, had no time to philosophize. When he stared up at the towering sides it seemed as though the boat deck rail and the lifeboats were "rushing" to crash down on him.

He called a steward over to help him tie the lifebelt, then put his money, about forty dollars, in the top of his sock. He bent over to take off his shoes, but decided there wasn't even time for that. The water was about twelve feet below his deck when he jumped, and he hit with a splash.

Archie felt its chilling drenching shock. Then the buoyant lifebelt brought him quickly back to the surface. Much to his surprise, swimming was "the most marvelous revelation." He had the illusion of skimming over the top of the water with incredible speed and ease, while the life preserver held his head and chest high.

He kept stroking, with one motivating desire—to get away from the ship.

Close by, a group of men who had already struggled onto a raft were huddled together like soaked terriers and singing, weakly, "Tipperary."

Herbert Ehrhardt reminded himself to keep his mouth shut as he hit the water. He must also keep eyes open and swim up toward the light whichever way the currents turned him, he thought. Then he jumped. There was at first a sensation of going farther and farther from the light in spite of swimming toward it . . . sinking, deeper and deeper.

Then the water became brighter, he broke the surface—and he was breathing again. His lungs ached. And he saw the turmoil was not yet over, for a huge wave was bearing an empty lifeboat at him.

The chemistry student raised his arms over his head to shield himself. The wave and boat passed, and he was sucked under once more. Again he struggled upward for the light, which became gradually brighter, lighter—and, finally, fresh air again filled his lungs. Now he had surfaced in an area of relative calm. He relaxed, floating quietly to catch his breath.

Matt Freeman, the British boxing champion, was in a hurry to get off, once his hand had been treated by Marie de Page. He ran to the stern, now the highest part of the ship.

When he looked down, he wondered if it weren't a bit too high.

Being an athlete in peak trim, he had full self-confidence. He climbed onto the railing and dove. He struck the side of a floating lifeboat. The blow opened a deep gash in his head and he could feel the blood ooze, even under water. But it had not knocked him out, and he began to swim.

Robert Wiemann thought "a second torpedo" hit about this time. Since the liner appeared to be sinking by the bow, he knew he could do no more for the passengers. He climbed onto the stern railing in the wake of Matt Freeman, and was awe-struck by the belief that it must be a hundred feet down to the water. He plunged anyhow.

When he surfaced, two men grabbed at him, so he had to duck beneath the surface again to free himself.

Thomas Mahoney, the seaman, concluded there was little more assistance he could give in lowering boats. He made for the stern and started to lower himself into the water by a rope, sailor-fashion. Halfway down he realized he was over the propellers; it looked to him as though they were still revolving slowly. He had a terrible choice—dropping between the blades or clambering back onto the deck.

He decided to "swarm" back up the rope. With considerable difficulty he shinnied up again, inch by inch, until he had finally gained the stern deck. This time he climbed onto the rail, gauged his distance down, and dove.

When he came to the surface, jarred but unhurt, he swam for a raft.

Others were jumping right after him, as though the ship's stern had turned into some macabre, monster springboard. Thomas Madden, the fireman who had finally struggled up through the ventilator, was among them. So was Frank

Tower, the fireman who had swum away from the *Titanic* and the *Empress of Ireland.* It had assumed the character of a fearsome routine.

Another fireman arrived abruptly on the deck having been blown, by some lesser internal explosion, the last few feet through an escape hatch. He was sooty, bruised, and bleeding but alive. He took one look at the angle of the ship and dove over the side. Many of the engine room crew were badly scalded, presenting an appearance that stuck in many minds as far more frightful than any other aspect of the nightmare.

Passengers plunged in and swam alongside the crewmen. Fifteen-year-old Virginia Bruce Loney, whose father had returned for her from ambulance driving in France, was among them—though involuntarily—as was Florence Padley. Each had been toppled into the water by an overturned lifeboat.

Virginia Bruce was a proficient swimmer. With fast, graceful strokes she swam away from the listing ship. As she turned her head she saw her mother and father. They were standing by the rail, beside their friend, Alfred Vanderbilt, who had helped her into the lifeboat.

It hurt her deep inside with an unfathomable helplessness to look at them. She knew she would never see them again.

Lieutenant Lasseter had the same feeling as he looked back from the water to see the sturdy figure of his friend, Commander Stackhouse, standing calmly on the stern.

Avis Dolphin was also swimming. She had not remained long in the lifeboat in which Professor Holbourn had placed her. Two men had jumped into it as it touched the water, capsizing it.

She had the feeling that she was the only one to have struggled clear of the upturned boat. Soon she spied a raft nearby, with people rowing. Two other men pulled her aboard.

Some distance from her, Holbourn himself was swimming with all his might. After he first jumped, he had trouble fighting through the jumble of ropes snarling the water around the liner, like submarine nets. Once free of them, he knifed ahead like a seventy-five-yard dash professional. He thought fleetingly of the curious prophetic dreams of such a disaster he had experienced several times in New York before sailing.

Others, not necessarily old or infirm, would not jump in spite of any amount of persuasion. Patrick L. Jones, London staff photographer and reporter with the International News Service, was one of them.

Charles T. Jeffrey, a Kenosha, Wisconsin, automobile man-ufacturer, spied Jones on the starboard side of B Deck. His arm wrapped around a stanchion, he balanced himself fur-ther with a foot against the rail. He was taking pictures as fast as he could load and focus his camera.

"You better get off this boat!" Jeffrey shouted.

"These'll be the greatest pictures ever!" replied Jones, not pausing to look at the other man.

Jeffrey thought it "the coolest thing" he would ever see, then hastened along the deck. He was uncertain whether to jump or look for a collapsible.

Theodate Pope had abandoned hope of obtaining space in a boat for herself and Edwin Friend. As she and Emily Rob-inson waited for him to return with the belts, it became obvious the great Cunarder was about finished: the ship—so vast it needed telephones to connect the cabins, so ornate that the Senator from Utah thought it "more beautiful than Solomon's Temple (and big enough to hold all his wives)"— would surely sink soon.

Friend tied the belts on the women, and they stood by the

ropes on the outer side of the deck in the place one of the
boats had occupied. They looked up at the leaning funnels
and could see the ship move. "She was going rapidly."

Now they could see the gray hull, once hidden, where the
waterline began. It looked like the underbelly of a great
whale.

It was time to jump.

"You go first," Theodate said.

Friend stepped over the ropes, slipped down one of the
uprights, and reached the rail of B Deck, next lower. Then
he jumped. The two women waited for Friend to come up.

In a few seconds they were relieved to see his head bobbing
in the foamy water, then he smiled to encourage them.

"Come, Robinson," Theodate said and stepped over the
ropes as Edwin Friend had before her. She slipped a short
distance, found a foothold on a roll of the canvas used for
deck shields, then jumped. She feared that her maid would
not follow her.

She could not reach the surface. She was being washed and
whirled up against something that felt like wood. Then she
opened her eyes and blinked in the green water—through the
murk it looked as though she were being dashed up against
a lifeboat keel.

"This of course is the end of life for me," she thought as
she closed her eyes again. She flailed her arms in a half-spir-
ited attempt to come to the surface. She thought of her
mother and was glad she had made a will. She started to count
all the buildings she designed—the ones built and building—
and hoped she had "made good."

Quietly she thought of the friends she loved, then committed herself, in "a prayer without words," to God's care.
She received a sudden blow on the head, felt it crashing

through the straw hat she still wore, and lapsed into unconsciousness.

As with Matt Freeman, the boxer, and Theodate Pope,
striking objects proved as deadly a menace as the cold ocean.
Ever since the *Lusitania* was hit, the waters were being increasingly choked with a strange, vast outpouring of debris:
crushed, splintered lifeboats, deck chairs, shoring lumber—
the awe-struck passengers did not know where it had all
come from.

Dr. Houghton remembered hitting his head as he went
underneath. The force of the water separated him from
Marie de Page. He looked back for a moment, saw her struggling, then she was swept away. He lost sight of her.

On deck, Dr. Fisher returned from his quest with two lifebelts.

"I had to wade through deep water to get them," he reported to Lady Mackworth and Dorothy Conner. This news
shocked them into action.

Margaret Mackworth unhooked her skirt so that it would
come straight off in the water and not impede her. She
watched the list of the *Lusitania*. She, as others, kept thinking it could not possibly lean over any farther. But it continued to list.

"I think we better jump into the sea," Dr. Fisher said
anxiously. As he eyed the nearing waters, he wondered how
the ship was keeping afloat at such a crazy angle.

Dr. Fisher and Dorothy moved to a place vacated by a
lifeboat, as Theodate and Edwin Friend had done before.
But there was no railing to impede them.

Margaret Mackworth followed a few paces behind, trying
to summon courage for the sixty-foot jump from the boat
deck to the water. She became more and more frightened. It

was like leaping off a rooftop. She held tightly onto the extra
lifebelt she still carried for her father.

"It is ridiculous to have a physical fear of the jump," she
tried to reassure herself, "when we are in such grave danger!"

She saw others hesitating at the edge of the boat deck and
reasoned they must have had the same fear. Then suddenly
the water washed over the deck, and she realized she was no
longer sixty feet above the ocean. In the next instant green
water was swirling around her knees.

That was as far as she remembered its rising. Then she
was engulfed by it.

Somewhere below, the little group that had been holding
tightly onto one another—Frohman, Rita Jolivet, Captain
Scott, and Vernon—had just been forcibly separated by the
crush of water. The wave that smashed, frothing, into them
seemed to be bearing other struggling, screaming people
along with it.

Its force tore Rita Jolivet's buttoned shoes off. Like Frohman she had made up her mind to die and she was "quite
calm under the water."

"The thought of God came to me—how at a time like this
He was everyone's God, a living, warm, all-pervading Presence. . . . The petty bickerings of creed and doctrine seemed
so foolish, so futile . . ."

She was distinctly surprised when the water brightened
and she floated to the surface. She reached for an upturned
lifeboat and clung to it, along with at least thirty other persons, who had apparently upset it.

Others splashed over and clung desperately to the keel.
The boat sank lower and lower.

Rita was seized with panic. Though she thought she had

resigned herself to dying, she now wanted to live. And she was faced a second time with death.

In the wheelhouse, with its port windows pointing crazily up at the blue sky, and starboard ones awash in the sea, Captain Turner did not want to die either.

Quartermaster Hugh Johnston had sung out:

"T-w-e-n-t-y f-i-v-e degrees!" and from then on the brass indicator swung steadily to starboard. It was little use for Johnston to try to keep up with it by singing out successive lists.

Turner watched the helm and the indicator with a darkening expression. Finally he said flatly to his quartermaster: "Save yourself."

Johnston left the helm and hurried over to the starboard bridge wing for a lifebuoy. It wouldn't be long, he thought, before he was washed right off this ship. He had never known anyone so "cool" as Captain Turner.

Marconi Operator Leith, now drenched in sweat, tirelessly flashing the SOS, knew the ship was going down. He could hardly hang onto his transmitter because of the list. Now, frantically, he altered the call:

SEND HELP QUICKLY. AM LISTING BADLY!

Walther Schwieger didn't think it would be long either. Aboard the *U-20*, he was recording:

3:25 P.M. It seems as if the vessel will be afloat only a short time. Submerge to 24 meters and go to sea. I could not have fired a second torpedo into this throng of humanity attempting to save themselves . . .

Just outside of the *Lusitania*'s radio shack, with its outjuttings of wires and insulators, Oliver Bernard had finished untying his shoes. Although he had thought himself to be practically alone, when he looked up he saw George Hutchinson, the chief electrician, at the door of the shack talking to Leith.

"What about it, Bob?" Hutchinson asked Leith.

Before Leith could answer, an engineer ran across the deck balancing himself against the list.

"The watertight doors are all right, quite all right, don't worry," the engineer reported, breathless, to Hutchinson.

The three men grinned at each other as the engineer moved along, and the electrician reassured Bernard, "Any amount of other ships about."

The scenic artist scanned the horizon without seeing a sign of a ship, and replied, "That doesn't interest me much. I can't swim a yard and that's not enough."

Inside his cubicle, Bob Leith stood up. He pushed his swivel chair out of the door toward Bernard. He told him it would be something to hang onto later.

"No good at working water-wheels either," Bernard said. The men all laughed as the chair careened down the sloping deck and crashed against the starboard rails.

Bernard found it difficult to stand at all. The list had increased alarmingly and the bow was nearly submerged.

The wireless operator ceased sending the distress message. Now he produced a small camera and, balancing himself uncertainly on his knees, took a picture looking forward.

"What a snap this will make!" he observed to Bernard.

The men looked away from the ship and distinguished one lifeboat among the others, about a mile away, making for the clearly visible shore. There appeared to be one lady, children, and an officer in this boat, which was being rowed by sailors. The sun glinted from the gold braid on the officer's sleeve—and Bernard, the electrician and the radioman all looked at each other in bitter understanding.

It was time for them to go too. The trio, as if by unexpressed agreement, started down to the starboard rails, half sliding as they went.

To Bernard it appeared that the *Lusitania* was about to roll over and carry with her all who remained aboard. He climbed over the stairway rails and down outside them. He dropped feet first onto the boat deck, facing inward. His rubber-soled boots, which he still wore, untied, kept him from tumbling over.

The edge of the deck was awash as he slipped toward it. A lifeboat floated nearby, held by the tackle of a single davit. He recognized it as Number 2, the first of the several which had dumped their passengers into the sea. Now it held new occupants, and Bernard splashed over to them, and into the boat.

Bernard helped others into the lifeboat. Among them was D. A. Thomas, who had been looking for his daughter, Margaret Mackworth, ever since the torpedo had struck. Both men then assisted a hysterical woman into the boat and halted the descent of a young boy who had made a flying leap.

The ropes from the davit were threatening to hold the lifeboat to the *Lusitania* and carry it down with her. Just in time, someone produced an ax and hacked the falls clear.

Hardly had that peril been eliminated than an incredible new danger presented itself. The liner was listing so far that the boat was caught on one of the steel funnel stays. The funnel overhung the tiny boat, threatening to tear loose and smash everyone "like flies" or at best smother them under its massive breadth—wide enough, as the advertisements lyricized, "to drive a coach and horses through."

All hands joined in a mighty effort which finally resulted
in pushing the boat clear of the "tentacle"-like funnel stay . . .
they watched the great liner sliding slowly away from them
downward.

It looked as though she were literally going to sink under
them, like a monster fish bent on a final, mighty plunge back
to the depths.

At this point Quartermaster Hugh Johnston was picked up
from the starboard side of the bridge, like a swimmer caught
in the tide, and washed all the way across the ship. He barely
missed ventilators, fans, stay wires, valveheads, and other ob-
structions.

On the other side of the bridge, which was almost completely awash, Turner glanced at his watch. It was 2:28 P.M.,
exactly eighteen minutes after the *Lusitania* had been hit.
He thought himself to be the last man on the ship—though
he was not—and realized that in a few more seconds he would
no longer have a command.

Here was the nightmare moment in the existence of a captain; this was ultimate heartbreak, world's end. In one instant, the planet-like substance and enduring solidity of a
32,000-ton liner; in the next, nothing, or perhaps eternity.

Turner was in full uniform, including his cap, with the
gold "scrambled eggs" on the visor. On the sleeve of his coat
the four wide gold stripes were tinged with the green of the
sea air but still impressive.

He would go down, if he must, in courage, in pride, a
man—and a Briton.

The deck assumed an impossible angle beneath him and
the water surged over his legs, the green, cold, relentless
water that was ruining forever the wonderful machinery of

his bridge, his helm, his brass telegraph to the engine room. . . .

He pulled his cap tighter around his head so it would not come off, and started to climb a ladder leading from the bridge to the signal halyards. Les Morton, who had spotted the torpedo (or two parallel torpedo tracks, he was increasingly certain) and was now in the water swimming away from a capsized boat, looked back in time to see Turner by the halyards. Stroking for his own life as he was, it struck him as a most dramatic sight, the captain with his ship to the very last.

Now, like the apprentice of sailing-ship days, Will Turner clutched instinctively for rigging, higher, higher. The tar rolled off into the palms of his hands, and its familiar pungent smell awakened in him a nostalgia he had tried to keep dormant. Memories of long-ago, better days, flashed dizzily before him.

He wondered what in God's name he had done to deserve this.

The huge Cunarder trembled under his grasp. He heard strange, watery eruptions far below as though they emanated from the ocean's very bed. Above him the skies were blue and bright . . . from the almost horizontal funnels a bare trace of coal smoke wisped redolently upward . . . a sea gull wheeled past.

He saw an oar floating toward him. He quit the rigging and struck out for it. He grabbed it, then let go and splashed over to a bobbing chair. He held onto the chair.

His cap remained on his head as he looked back at his ship. The funnels and mast tips seemed to be righting, swinging in a slow arc back toward the zenith, just where they should be pointing. An all-swallowing wave foamed past the base of the funnels, over the Marconi deck, over what remained above water of the boat deck, like heavy surf after a storm. It was one long comber.

From the stern, now that her bow was buried beneath the water, those still aboard the *Lusitania* had a fleeting and bizarre perspective. It was one which they realized, even then, was unlikely to be duplicated in the infinity of time.

As the liner tilted sharply downward, the fantail soared a hundred feet into the air, exposing four nearly motionless propellers, as well as the immense sixty-five-ton rudder. And to complete the nightmare, she stopped there, frozen still, her forward motion suddenly and strangely arrested.

Those who dared not jump from the stern because of the height—including men like C. T. Jeffrey, from Kenosha, and Parry Jones, one of the Royal Welsh singers—suspected the uncanny truth. Captain Turner, pausing to gasp a lungful of air, saw it!—his great ship, poised at an unbelievable angle, "quivered her whole length." Others who did not understand one nautical term knew only that the "point end" of the liner was jutting skyward, and seemed to hang there.

Sailor and landlubber alike realized that the *Lusitania,* nearly 800 feet from stem to stern, had already hit bottom.

The pride of Cunard, first superliner to be powered by steam turbines, ventilated by "thermo-tank," with elevators, telephones, electric chandeliers, roof gardens, tapestry, 175 watertight compartments, ocean greyhound that could race at more than twenty-five knots, beat the German steamers, outrun any enemy submarine, towering 216 feet from keel to mast tips, had slid through the 300-foot depth off the Irish coast, and stuck her towering bow fast in sand and mud.

Those on the steep mountain peak of her stern heard the

crashing from inside her superstructure, from her cargo spaces, engine rooms, throughout all the compartmented caverns of her stretching hull. It was as though a big hardware store had been turned upside down.

They stared below them at the swarms of men, women, and children twisting like flies and wrigglers on a lily pond, some on the surface, some just under, helpless human beings who did not know any more than Turner why God had done this to them.

The *Lusitania,* eleven miles from shore, 183 degrees, almost due south of the white lighthouse on the Old Head of Kinsale, was 270 miles from Liverpool. And she was over the same spot where a wallowing, unknown sailing schooner, the *Earl of Latham,* had been found by the submarine not many hours before.

Even Captain Turner had to admit the terrible truth—the mighty *Lusitania* shared a common mortality with all ships.

With increasingly ominous rumblings the liner began to right herself and settle lower by the stern. The wave rolled anew, flecking foam along the last exposed portions of her superstructure and decking. A few boats still hung, like broken toys, from davits.

One of the last boats that did get away carried Dr. Mecredy, who had pulled himself out of the water and over the stern. He was wet, his hands hurt and bleeding, but he was alive. Some fifty yards away, the *Lusitania's* stern and the propellers still loomed menacingly above him. He watched her settle, not quite certain what this amazing liner might do next.

Sculling a raft close to the doctor, Seaman Mahoney watched in similar fascination, with his own interpretation of the ship's actions. She was expressing, he thought, "glorious defiance," even in her death agonies.

The occupants of her fantail, C. T. Jeffrey, Parry Jones, and others, were reluctantly leaving their last tiny island of refuge, or preparing to do so.

From another lifeboat that had barely cleared the *Lusitania,* Elizabeth Duckworth looked out on a world the like of which she had never seen before. The sea was filled with bodies as well as an indescribable mass of debris, and it was "a terrible sight." To see dead men and women was one thing. When there were children, even infants—that was something for which she was prepared neither by faith nor training. Nor did she dare to think about the many more who must still be trapped in the deep, now-flooded world of steerage.

Loud enough for those seated beside her to hear, she finished the 23rd Psalm for the second time:

". . . for Thou art with me; Thy rod and Thy staff comfort me. Thou shalt prepare a table before me against them that trouble me; Thou hast anointed my head with oil, and my cup shall be full. But Thy loving kindness and mercy shall follow me all the days of my life; and I will dwell in the house of the Lord forever."

13

As Archie Donald coughed out a mouthful of water he looked behind him and saw the propellers and rudder of the *Lusitania* silhouetted in mid-air. A group of survivors, in a lifeboat, placed their oars against the lower propeller and pushed themselves off.

Then, with an "explosion and rattling of all the loose material leaving her deck," the ship gathered momentum for her last plunge. She appeared to be going down sideways, with her stern toward the shore, and Donald had a great fear the mast would hit him. At the same time he wondered, curiously, whether the stay ropes were made of hemp or wire.

Whatever their composition, the ropes missed him by less than fifteen feet. Then, a three-foot high wave picked Donald up and shot him out into the water that had been calm as a pond split seconds before. The suction of the vortex drew him down.

Archie swam against the current with a complete absence of fear that it would "get the better" of him. As he finally surfaced, an eight-by-eight-inch post and a two-by-six-inch plank—measured by his appraising eye—shot up alongside

166

like projectiles. Now he felt "guarded." He would undoubtedly have been decapitated had they been closer.

He reached the sturdy lumber which might have killed
him, and hung on.

Several passengers had safely abandoned the great liner
only to be met with another deadly—and not anticipated—
menace. It was the radio antenna, something which voyagers
had become accustomed to watching laced high against the
sky, some distance above even the funnels.

As the *Lusitania* tipped over, the wire caught Lauriat, for
one, around the shoulders and dragged him under. He would
not have been "as much surprised" if the submarine had
surfaced with him straddling its conning tower.

Miraculously, he fought clear of the aerial and surfaced
again, as did others, including Virginia Bruce Loney and
James Brooks. Most, however, were badly bruised by it.

When Brooks bobbed back up again, his hand stinging
from where the wire had cut in, he saw the *Lusitania*—
pointed dead for the land, he thought—going down "with
a thunderous roar as of the collapse of a great building
during a fire." He figured that at least some of the terrible
sound was caused by the turbines tearing loose from their
mountings and crashing into the bow.

It seemed to him that the ship sank sideways, still listing,
although Lauriat thought she had recovered "on quite an
even keel" as she settled by the stern. Turner himself estimated she came back to within five degrees of even keel.

Some, like Wiemann and Mahoney, of the crew, felt a
violent explosion after the *Lusitania* disappeared, as though
the boilers had exploded. Mahoney was sure a vapor covered
the sea momentarily before it dissipated. Wiemann was
impressed with the quiet that settled over the scene of in-

credible destruction, which took the pattern of "a circle of people and wreckage about half a mile across."

Lauriat, however, heard "a long, lingering moan" that rose and lasted many moments; "those who were lost seemed to be calling from the very depths." And others recalled it sounded like the waters were wailing in horror.

All saw the wave surge out from the spot where the *Lusitania* had plunged, bearing a threatening flotsam of deck chairs, oars, boxes, crushed boats, a nameless "deluge."

To Professor Holbourn the spot assumed the shape of "a pork pie"—a large, whitish broken mass, caused presumably by a final explosion. While the aerial did not endanger him, the after mast barely missed shattering a lifeboat close by. Then he struck out toward the boat, taking in tow a man who was floating beside him.

Oliver Bernard, from the relative security of a lifeboat, envisioned the scene as "a boiling wilderness that rose up as if a volcanic disturbance had occurred beneath a placid sea."

Dr. Mecredy, on the other hand, found that his boat rode away very nicely. He concluded there was little undertow.

Timmins went so far under that he never saw the *Lusitania*'s final moments of anguish. His last memories were of "Niagara Falls" as the superstructure bore him down with it. Soon the water around him was "black as the inside of a cow," and the top of his head felt like a "steel plate" from increasing pressure. Something struck the crown of his head.

He figured he was at least sixty feet below the surface, which was certainly fifty feet deeper than he had ever dived before. But he remained as methodical as ever. He kept count as he swam up, fighting away from the superstructure, taking exactly thirty-one strokes before he surfaced.

Then, after "seconds which seemed like hours," the black

changed to gray. Timmins blinked, looked around and figured
he was about 150 yards east of the main log jam of wreckage.
He was impressed by the calm—"no row, just a sort of hum
over the water."

A boy of about ten floated past in the tangle of bodies
and wreckage. There was no sound. He pressed his fingers
to the boy's ribs, but could detect no heart beat. Then he
raised his eyes from the still form and saw the smoke of a
steamer trailing across the horizon, passing on a westerly
course.

Alice Middleton, the baby's nurse from Seattle, was carried
far below. It seemed to her that her benefactor, Vanderbilt,
had been washed off the deck, without a lifebelt, before he
had finished securing hers. On the other hand, someone else
thought he had seen Vanderbilt light a cigarette and saunter
forward.

Beneath the surface, her head had become jammed in an
opened porthole and the pressure had made her eardrums
seem about to burst. It tortured her with a pain so great that
she did not see how she could endure, much less survive, it.

Yet, somehow, she returned to the surface, to be appalled
at once by the vast numbers of bodies—especially those of
children—floating all around her. They looked like drowned
dolls.

Beside her a woman was struggling. Alice stared in disbelief. The woman was giving birth to a baby, there in the
water, alone. It was the most terrible thing she had ever
witnessed—or would witness in her life. She became sick with
a pitying horror, helpless to do anything for the woman.
Soon Alice lost consciousness.

Margaret Gwyer, the bride of the Canadian minister, had
been knocked out of her boat and her companions had

already given her up for lost when she was scooped up by
one of the funnels along with a jumble of smashed wreckage.
She was sucked into it as the *Lusitania* went under.

The explosion shot her out again, as if from a cannon.
The minister's lady went into the air and down into the
water, landing a considerable distance from her boat and
her husband.

William H. Pierpont, of Liverpool, had the same bizarre
experience. He was swimming near Captain Turner when
the latter saw Pierpont suddenly swallowed by a disappearing funnel. Next the "Inspector," as Turner called the gentleman, shot forth again, while the "air rushed out with a
terrible hissing sound." Turner watched, incredulous, though
he obtained a measure of grim humor from the sight. As
Pierpont hit the water and struck out he seemed to be
"swimming like ten men, he was so scared."

The incident relieved only slightly Turner's deep sense
of loss. He knew now why the ship had heeled so terribly
after the torpedo hit: it was, paradoxically enough, her
very watertightness! With all her 175 hydraulically controlled watertight compartments, flooding between port and
starboard sides had not been equalized. Not until moments
before the end had the force of thousands of tons of water
apparently burst through the damlike fore-and-aft bulkhead.

This very aspect of marine engineering had contributed
to the debacle of lifeboat launching, compounding the terror
and transforming his graceful command into a plunging,
careening monster. She had been somewhat top-heavy, too, it
occurred to Turner; her nine decks made her like a hotel
with too many stories. Yet not until the *Lusitania* had been
stricken with her mortal wounds had this fact caused any

particular comment other than to give the liner the reputa-
tion of a "roller" in the minds of queasy passengers.

Will Turner hung onto his chair, dogpaddling slowly.
He watched the mound of boiling water slowly dwindling
to bubbles. Then the bubbles too disappeared and the sea
was calm again.

Nothing remained of the *Lusitania* but a clutter of boats,
debris, and people.

In eighteen minutes the liner had been utterly destroyed—
obliterated, as if it had never existed, a modern Carthage.

George Kessler, sometimes called the "champagne king,"
stared from his boat at the same foaming spot, then after
a few moments pronounced his own startled benediction:

"My God—the *Lusitania*'s gone!"

It was even as Hubbard had written about the *Titanic*:
"the great iron monster slips, slides, gently glides, surely,
down, down, down into the sea. Where once the great ship
proudly floated, there is now a mass of wreckage, the dead,
the dying."

But who was there now to write of Elbert Hubbard or
Alice Hubbard and the "great iron monster," *Lusitania?*
Where was the Fra, where was Alice?

That puzzled Ernest Cowper as he searched the faces in
the water round his boat. He could have sworn he saw the
Hubbards walking down a passageway and into one of the
cabins—in those last few moments. And Lauriat could not
understand how in the world they had left that corner of the
deck and disappeared into the air.

C. T. Hill, Richmond and London tobacco man, who
had been dumped from one of the improperly launched
boats, thought he had seen the East Aurora couple in that
same boat. Lott Gadd, the popular barber friend of Froh-

man, in charge of that lifeboat, didn't think they had been his passengers. And someone else thought he recognized Hubbard struggling alone in the water in a vain effort to cling to a cylindrical steel drum; still another that Hubbard had been trapped under a funnel.

Yet even a trained and objective reporter like Cowper admitted that no one viewing that crazy scene could really be sure of anything any more—of even the familiar face of the homespun bard, with the Buster Brown haircut, who made people happy with little sayings and actions.

From shore the sinking was somewhat like a toy boat toppling over in a swan pond. To young Murphy the *Lusitania* "just seemed to get lower in the water and finally disappear." Others, including a child named Constance Karney, recalled the "boom" of what they thought were the boilers exploding. The signal station at Kinsale placed the time at 2:33 P.M.

American Consul Wesley Frost, in his dingy second-floor consulate above a Queenstown bar, heard the first word about that time. He cranked up the telephone and called Paymaster Norcocks in Admiral Coke's headquarters, and received confirmation of what he did not want to hear:

"It's true, Mr. Frost. We fear she's gone."

It was almost impossible to believe. The local Cunard agent, J. J. Murphy, acted like a man in a dream. He quickly started the preliminaries: made hotel arrangements, mustered the volunteer first-aid corps, sent a signal to London, notified doctors and the Royal Hospital, and alerted the mortuaries.

The whole south Irish coast was alive with the news. Pinpoints like Courtmacsherry and Clonakilty, Ross Carbery and Oysterhaven seethed with excitement. On the three-mile outjut of the Old Head of Kinsale itself people began to congregate at Ringarteen, Bay West, Ringalurisky Point, Black Head, Bullens Bay, and Kitchen Point, even close to sea-washed Bream Rock—just waiting, and watching the rescue boats beating to the scene.

Frost saw the beginnings of the "mosquito fleet" steam past the town as he began his hasty preparations, pondering all the while what Secretary of State William Jennings Bryan would say to *this*.

To the west of Queenstown, in the water, survivors like Archie Donald were trying to get organized too. He hung onto his lumber until he saw a pile of collapsible boats. He swam to them and was hauled aboard. The first man he saw was one of his roommates, George Bilbrough, of Smith Falls, Canada. The two went to work and succeeded in raising the canvas sides of one boat.

Soon they had four women and four men aboard. Mme N. M. Papadapoulo, separated from her husband, had been in the water almost twenty minutes without a lifebelt. The Greek lady was swimming around with her dress on and Donald was amazed that she had not become hopelessly waterlogged. Another woman, who could not swim, had been clinging to a deck chair and seemed in generally good shape. Olive North was brought in behind her.

Donald considered Miss T. Winter, of New York, to be one of the bravest women he had ever seen. She had been swept off the ship while her arm was locked around the canvas cover of a collapsible. Unable to swim and helpless without a lifebelt, she was borne along by the moving flotsam. Clad only in a thin petticoat and blouse, she was bleeding from gashes in her head and back when rescued. Even so she went to work giving artificial respiration to others, and succeeded in saving several lives. Although he was sure he had walked across her bare feet a number of times, she did not once complain.

They filled the boat with thirty-four men and women and still the water was black with hundreds of people. Every available piece of wreckage was covered with the living as well as the dead and the dying.

It was a "most terrible thing to see the people struggling for their lives." Donald wished with all his heart he could help more. But the bow of his collapsible had been damaged and he dared not bring others aboard lest they swamp the none-too-seaworthy boat.

His crew appeared "most motley." Almost no one knew how to row or steer. One troublesome individual kept shouting about his money and his bonds. He finally became "such a nuisance" that Donald hit him on the head with an oar. That quieted him and he sulked.

Donald wondered if they could ever reach the lighthouse toward which he was setting a rough course.

Meanwhile, Lorna Pavey, whom he had left eating a grape-fruit in Second Class dining saloon, was having her own troubles. She had obeyed the Reverend Gwyer implicitly and stayed where she was till the dining room was almost empty. Donald's card-playing roommate, John Wilson, spied her there when he finished helping close the ports.

He had grabbed her by the hand and half pulled her through the deepening mounds of flowers, silver, broken crockery, and glassware. They had been forced to walk up the staircase on the rungs of a bannister as the steps were at almost a 45-degree angle, then to C Deck, where Wilson spotted a boat already lowered and half full of water as well as people. He told her to slide down a rope.

Miss Pavey had an interesting descent. Her ample skirt ballooned out and she almost floated onto the water. Wilson followed and they rolled over the gunwale into the boat. Now they were bailing furiously with their shoes, for no one had noticed the plug was out until the boat was almost swamped.

At the same time they were trying to persuade the hard-bitten group of firemen who were rowing the boat to stop and pick up others. With only twelve aboard, there was plenty of room. But the rowers refused to heed the request.

On the other hand, Leslie Morton and another seaman, William Parry, were rapidly hauling people onto their collapsible. When they had saved about fifty persons, they rowed off toward what looked like a fishing ketch, about five miles distant.

They were impressed with one crew member in particular. Kathleen Kaye, the fourteen-year-old girl who had been en route home from a visit to New York, handled an oar like a man. When not rowing, she helped fill the boat, comforted survivors, and administered first aid.

Theodate Pope had not fared so well. She regained consciousness in a "gray world." While the blow had been cushioned by her straw hat and her hair, it had temporarily affected her sight. She could not see sunlight although she was certain that she was on the surface.

Gradually she became aware that she was surrounded and jostled by hundreds of frantic, screaming humans in her "watery inferno." A man, insane with fright, had affixed himself to her shoulders. Half dazed as she was, Theodate recognized the panic in his eyes as he stared wildly over her head. He had no lifebelt and his weight was pulling her under again.

She was too tired to struggle against him, which might have made him cling all the more tightly.

"Oh, please don't," she implored. Then the water closed over her and she lapsed back into unconsciousness.

When she opened her eyes a second time she was floating on her back, staring into brilliant sunlight and blue sky. The man had gone. Other men and women were floating about her, but at increasing distances. She noticed a man on her right with a gash on his forehead; close by she could make out the back of a woman's head. At her left was a peculiar sight—"an old man upright in the water." His life jacket must have been exceptionally buoyant for he was treading water.

Since he seemed to occupy an elevated position, with the horizon surely in his sight, she asked him:

"Do you see any rescue ships coming?"

He said, "No," after a look around.

An Italian with his arms girdling a small tin tank floated by, chanting. There were occasional shouts, and somewhere in the background the discordant singing of "Tipperary."

Ship's boats, far away, all appeared crowded. Theodate wondered where Edwin Friend was. The water felt warm and it occurred to her she might be able to remain afloat some time. Then an oar bobbed by; she took hold of one end, pushing the other to the old man who was half standing at her left.

Now the increasing weight of her soaked clothes was dragging her down. She lifted her right foot over the oar blade and held it with her left hand. This improved her buoyancy and she did not have to exhaust her dwindling energy to keep afloat.

She tried to raise her head to see if rescue were on the

way. Then she sank back, wearied from the effort. Thinking
it "too horrible to be true," she soon lost consciousness.

Near her Rita Jolivet's upturned boat, which had almost
been swamped anew by too many clinging people, had just
been bolstered by another collapsible which drifted under
the first and stuck there. As she caught her breath, Rita took
notice of her surroundings, even recognized a few familiar
faces—or thought she did, soot-stained as they were—such as
Dr. Fisher, from Washington. She was glad to see him, managed a weak smile.

Twice the cry had gone up, "Rescue ships coming!" making her think their "Gethesemane" was over, only to be
faced with cold disappointment. The second time she thought
she did see a boat or part of one heave in close, then disappear. She concluded it was a submarine that had surfaced
and submerged.

Others thought the same thing. A few swore they saw its
conning tower. Some, in their hysteria, believed the Germans
were firing deck guns, or cutting ropes spread between wreckage to which survivors were clinging.

Whatever the truth, Kapitan Schwieger, just about then,
entered in his log aboard the *U-20*:

> Go to 11 meters and take look around. In the distance
> astern are drifting a number of lifeboats. Of the *Lusitania*
> nothing is to be seen. The wreck must lie off Old Head of
> Kinsale Lighthouse, 14 sea miles distant, in 90 meters of water,
> 358 degrees (bearing to the lighthouse), 27 miles from Queens-
> town . . . 51° 22.6′, 8° 32′ W. The shore and lighthouse are
> clearly seen.

Aboard the ancient flagship *Juno*, Admiral Hood was debating whether to order Captain A. K. Macrorie to put back
into Queenstown. He had received the radio flash from Kin-

sale signal station that the *Lusitania* had sunk. There seemed no more need for their services: the other rescue boats would pick up survivors.

His four cruisers, anyhow, were worthless against a submerged U-boat. *Juno, Isis* and *Venus,* a bit over 5,000 tons, were 20 years old, mounted a main battery of 6" guns. *Sutlej,* only three years younger, was heavier, carried two 9.2-inch guns, yet was equally slow and ponderous in maneuvering.

The *Katerina,* a Greek "coaster" which had heard the SOS, kept on, along with the "mosquito fleet," and larger ships like the *Etonian, Narragansett,* and *City of Exeter.* A number of auxiliaries also had turned in the direction of the Old Head of Kinsale.

Many whom they hoped to save were still in the water, without even the shell-like protection of collapsibles. One of them, Matt Freeman, still dazed from striking his head on the lifeboat, was engaged in a macabre life-or-death struggle against five other men for finger room on a small keg.

Just before he had found the keg he had been submerged a second time by a man who grabbed him, "eyes bulging with fear."

The athlete had become faint with the effort to stay afloat. No match for the clawing mass of terrified men, he slipped away from the keg. He seized a passing deckchair and finally reached an upturned lifeboat to which a dozen people already clung.

In the hours that followed many dropped off. Half-conscious himself, he was aware that "ten of them died beside me there in the water."

The fears and physical suffering of many were heightened by a belief that they were drifting out to sea. Wiemann, the First Class saloon steward, sharing an upturned collapsible with ten other persons and one corpse, despaired of rescue. The shore appeared to be fading in the distance.

Captain Turner now noticed sea gulls swooping down toward him. He beat them off with his powerful arms, wondered if they were attacking, or simply curious.

Lady Margaret Mackworth clung desperately to a thin piece of board a few inches wide and two or three feet long. She was confident that it alone kept her afloat despite her well-fastened lifebelt.

She soon formed part of a "large, round floating island of people and debris," all compactly together. In addition to boards and chairs, sharing ocean space with the people were a number of hencoops, minus their recent occupants.

A man with a white face and a yellow mustache took hold of the other end of her diminutive board. It was scarcely large enough for two, but she did not feel "justified" in objecting. He tried to move around to her end of the board and it frightened her.

Finally she summoned her strength, for it had become an effort to speak, and told him to go back to his own end of the board. Shortly after that he disappeared, and she never saw him again, although she had the vague notion he may have climbed aboard a hencoop.

Many were praying aloud in a "curious, unemotional monotone," while Margaret Mackworth heard others shouting for help in a slow chant,

"Bo-at . . . bo-at . . . bo-at . . . !"

She joined the chorus a minute or two until its uselessness became obvious. She saw one or two boats but they had all they could do to pick up the bobbing people close by them.

Her legs became "bitterly" cold, but she decided to try to swim to a boat. After a few strokes she gave up, exhausted.

The slim board seemed her only salvation and she floated in the water, clutching it, "which nothing would have induced me to abandon."

She was conscious of no acute feeling of fear, but extremely thankful she had not drowned, trapped beneath the surface. So long as her head was out of water she felt there could be nothing unbearable, "even if the worst happened." Too, she was becoming accustomed to the rather comfortable position in which the lifebelt held her, with her head slightly back, as though lying in a hammock.

She doubted that the others were any more frightened than she since immersion in the cold water tended to make one "a little dazed and rather stupid and vague." Like Theodate Pope, she had the feeling the whole thing was a nightmare from which she would soon awake. She looked at the sun, blue skies, and calm seas and asked herself if perchance she had reached heaven unawares—and immediately hoped not.

Soon she became less comfortable, both from the numbing water and from a slight swell which made her seasick. She was seized with the idea that lifebelts should be equipped with a small bottle of chloroform so a person could inhale and mercifully lose consciousness in moments like this.

The swell drifted her island of wreckage apart until she noticed she was a hundred yards or more away from the nearest person. It induced a feeling of loneliness. She felt drowsy . . .

Hymn singing drifted over the water, first the mournful, beseeching strains of "Abide with Me" and shortly afterwards "Nearer My God to Thee." Some recognized the professional quality—the same Royal Gwent singers who had sung the "Star-Spangled Banner" at the sailing in New York and given a concert in each saloon during the crossing. Four surviving members of the Welsh Male Chorus had been reunited on an upturned boat.

When Professor Holbourn reached his boat, he found the man he was towing was dead. He let him go.

The boat was crowded and the petty officer in charge decided they would try to reach an almost empty one about three quarters of a mile distant. Rowing was difficult. The boat was jammed. They finally made it, even so, and were greeted by two men, naked except for military blankets.

Holbourn remained in the first boat, overloaded even after the transfer of fifteen passengers. He was feeling revived from the sunshine and the effort of rowing, although he still shivered.

As his boat continued toward shore, they went through seeming endless fields of wreckage, strung out as an indication of the curving shoreward track of the stricken *Lusitania*. Large numbers of drowning people were "shrieking for help," but the petty officers in charge of the boat "refused" to assist them. Holbourn believed they could "with absolute safety" have taken aboard at least ten more persons.

What especially appalled the professor was the sight of some thirty bodies drowned because their lifebelts were improperly worn. Now he remembered bitterly the deputation from the male passengers and his "Ostrich Club." George Hutchinson, the chief electrician, swam by a man in this predicament whom he took to be Vanderbilt. Hutchinson tried to adjust the belt there in the water, but found it an impossible task. They drifted apart.

Meanwhile, as Holbourn's boat pulled toward shore, the rowers sighted a fishing smack. They increased their efforts.

Brooks found a collapsible and was joined by a husky seaman and another man. The three of them took out jackknives and went to work assembling the canvas sides of the collapsible boat.

The operation was tedious and further complicated by struggling survivors who kept clinging to the shallow gunwales, like barnacles. The three tried vainly to persuade them to hang onto the lifelines around the collapsible instead, so they would not obstruct the work on the sides, which were difficult enough to lock in place.

With the sides down, a collapsible resembles a dory-shaped raft—and even that looked good enough to those who feared themselves on the brink of drowning.

All Brooks received were cries of despair whenever he attempted to explain the difficulties. People fancied he was trying to push them off to drown. Once the sides were up, the seats had to be slid into place; next the men had to fish around in the wreckage for oars. Finally, with an added 200-pound recruit plus the recently arrived Charles Lauriat, they had a fully manned skiff. As they commenced rowing, they heard a cry.

The men reached over and grabbed the outstretched hands of a woman they took for an African. There were no white spots on her except her teeth and the whites of her eyes. She was bruised and her clothes were almost torn off!

"I'm Margaret Gwyer," she identified herself.

Her story of being projected from the funnel seemed incredible, but no one questioned it. One's sense of proportion had been altered in the past half hour.

Another woman stroked toward the boat, pushing aside bodies like so many lily pads on a peaceful pond. Brooks noted objectively how well her hair was in place, how "beautifully" she swam.

"Won't you take me next?" was the cool request from

another woman, floating just ahead of the lifeboat and too
jammed in by packing crates to free her arms. Her hair
streamed out over the surrounding wreckage and she was
placidly chewing gum. Lauriat thought she sounded as un-
concerned as though she were asking "for a slice of bread
and butter."

Her wool skirt had absorbed pounds of water, but finally
the men hauled her aboard. She sat down, brushed her hair
back, and continued chewing gum.

A couple of redheaded Cockney stokers, completing the
crew, joined the rowers and kept up an outspoken com-
mentary which the others considered was "something to
remember." The collapsible was pushed through the now-
clearing waters toward the lighthouse. It seemed an infinite
distance, even though the light stood out sharp and white.

Shortly the sail of a fishing vessel appeared dead ahead.
Just then they came abreast of a man swimming all by himself.

"I'm off on my own," he explained, politely refusing a lift.

Yet the boat had not pulled ahead many yards before the
man changed his mind and yelled. Around him was one of
the *Lusitania*'s few big round white lifebuoys, which could
have protected him almost indefinitely from sinking, but the
chill had become too much to endure.

L. McMurray, of Toronto, as he introduced himself, was
blue when pulled aboard the collapsible. Ship disasters were
not new to him, for he had been aboard the White Star
liner *Republic* in 1909 when it was rammed off Nantucket
Light. CQD, predecessor of SOS, had flashed across the radio
waves that January Saturday evening to start a new chapter
in the history of sea rescues.

Soon McMurray thawed sufficiently to lend a hand with the oars as they pushed toward the fishing smack.

Herbert Ehrhardt, when he had caught his breath, saw he was next to an upturned boat with the two brothers who had been his cabin mates. Another boat, right side up, was lying partly across the first.

The younger of the pair climbed into the righted boat. In the maneuver the craft separated, leaving one of the brothers on each boat. Ehrhardt and the older of the two began to help people onto the bottom of their boat. One woman, who had been gasping for breath, died a few moments after being pulled aboard.

Herbert was impressed at the speed with which the boat became separated from other boats and pieces of wreckage. The one with the younger brother on it was completely out of sight.

When the upturned craft was almost full, an extremely exhausted man was helped on. For some minutes he lay there, struggling for his breath, unable to lift his head from the wet planking. When finally he looked around he gave a low moan and buried his head against the planking again, sobbing.

The dead woman, still lying across the boat, was his wife.

A little later a corpse in a life jacket floated past. Ehrhardt half raised it out of the water on the chance it may have been someone he knew. It was. And his cabin mate, next to him, recognized the corpse too. It was the cabin mate's father.

It had turned into a grim load on Ehrhardt's upturned lifeboat. Their gloom was in no way alleviated when they watched a small steamer come close and then apparently continue on its way. But it wasn't too long before numerous

columns of smoke appeared on the horizon, then grew steadily in size. Finally a vessel which Ehrhardt thought was a
destroyer came within hailing distance and asked if they were
all right.

"Yes!" Ehrhardt shouted back.

The vessel, the auxiliary *Indian Prince,* promised to come
back for them later.

Oliver Bernard, in his boat, also lifted a dead woman
from the waters. Along with the saloon deck steward, some
stokers, and trimmers, he was pulling on an oar when a
woman's face, "as green as the sea," drifted past his gunwale.
They brought her into the bottom of the boat, propped her
shoulders against Bernard's knees.

He shook his head, knowing it was too late to revive her.
With a frothy mucous on her lips she peered blindly ahead.

Oliver "awkwardly" helped the others to row. Presently
they sighted a fishing smack inshore, completely becalmed.
On their way they took two more lifeboats and a raft in tow,
until they looked like a small train meandering at snail's
pace across the sea.

It made rowing difficult, with the massive deadweight now
added astern. But neither the scenic artist nor anyone else
could object—they were bringing 150 souls to safety. And all
the while the "Blue Danube" still supplied a bizarre musical
background in Bernard's mind.

Elizabeth Duckworth was too busy to pray. Soon after her
lifeboat pulled away from the sinking *Lusitania,* she noticed
a man struggling in the water and asked the petty officer in
charge:

"Can't we help him?"

"No," he replied.

"Yes, we can," Elizabeth snapped back.

This time the officer took a longer look at the weaver from
Taftville, at the square cut of her jaw, and ordered the
rowers to stop. It was a hard pull, but with the determined
Elizabeth and several strong men clutching at the man in the
water, they brought him in.

Her lifeboat started out for Queenstown. In spite of a
heavy load, it managed to make the fastest time of any of the
lifeboats. A foamy wake bubbled behind to attest its speed.
Mrs. Duckworth took her turns at the oars.

They did not row to Queenstown, but they were the first
to encounter the vanguard of the "mosquito fleet," *The Peel
12,* of Glasgow, the same becalmed trawler Lauriat and others
were making for. The fishermen shook their heads in solemn
disbelief as the sodden, half-clad survivors clambered over
the sides of their vessel.

Elizabeth had no sooner stepped aboard the craft—im-
mensely large after the lifeboat—than another lifeboat, with
but three persons in it, drifted within hailing distance. The
petty officer of her boat asked what had happened.

The answer came back that the boat had capsized and
all the others were in the water somewhere. The voice asked
for help to row back.

"I can't spare anyone," Elizabeth heard the officer call,
with a shake of his head.

Now the two craft, lifeboat, and *The Peel 12,* had drifted
close together. Elizabeth kept measuring the distance.

"You can spare me!" she suddenly blurted to the petty
officer. She held up her skirts and jumped across the few
feet of water separating her from the lifeboat. She landed in
it, and it bobbed under the impact but did not capsize.
Once again she rolled up the sleeves of her blouse and
reached for an oar.

14

Friday afternoon in New York was cloudy, mild, and somewhat humid. There was a presentiment of rain. From his fifth-floor room in Columbia University's newly constructed Furnald Hall, Ambrose Plamondon alternately pored through law books and glanced out of the window, past the two towering apartment houses across Broadway and at the Hudson River beyond. The vista whispered to him of distance, rekindled latent vagabond yearnings. He hadn't forgotten the French Foreign Legion.

He had just finished a Swiss cheese sandwich and a bottle of milk, purchased at the delicatessen on 116th Street. It was one-forty-five and a longer, more tedious afternoon ahead than he relished, before the evening's auditorium concert: Grieg's Concerto and a bit of Tschaikowsky. Otherwise the day would be sacrificed in a juridical miasma of Blackstone.

It was not long after he had noted the time that his room buzzer rang. He stood up, happy at the unexpected distraction, and padded out and down the dormitory hallway. He picked up the wall phone in the small end closet.

"Am?" came the shaken voice of Harry Askin, manager of

the Grand Theater and long-time friend of the family. "I was just over to the *Herald*—they tell me the *Lusitania's* been sunk."

While not entirely unexpected, it was nonetheless stunning to Am.

"All right," he found himself answering rather flatly. "Will you let me know if you hear more?"

Automatically he returned to his desk. After sitting there for a moment, he put on his old tennis shoes and shuffled downstairs and out onto the campus. He blinked in the hazy glare of the May afternoon.

He looked back at the seven-story brick building, then at the statue of Thomas Jefferson to his left, the young elm tree on the other side of Furnald Hall, the dome of the nearby Cathedral of St. John the Divine towering over rooftops. The familiar sights swam before his eyes—and he realized he was in a daze. It came as a shock for him to find that he was not in complete emotional control.

Am continued across the soft spring grass of the campus toward the office of Professor John Barrett Moore, to see if he could be excused from his international law examinations.

The news—even as the waters off the south Irish coast were filled with struggling survivors—was met elsewhere in New York with varying reactions. In Hoboken crews of the tied-up German liners, including the giant *Vaterland,* had somehow heard it even before most newspapers and were drinking boisterous toasts in waterfront saloons.

The word was not received in other areas of Hoboken with the same joy. Two of its most distinguished residents, Ogden Hammond, former American diplomat, and his wife Mary were aboard the *Lusitania.*

In nearby Paterson, New Jersey, Billy Sunday had just

finished a sermon at the Tabernacle on "amusements" when a reporter told him the news. He burst into tears as he screamed to his startled audience:

"It's damnable, absolutely hellish!"

Charles P. Sumner, general agent for Cunard, had sat for an hour, too stunned to prepare his official announcement. His immobilization was augmented by recollection of the scenes at the rival White Star office when the *Titanic* went down three years ago. His counterparts, forced to meet grief-stricken relatives, had learned at first hand the stuff of which nightmares were woven.

Finally an intimate newspaper acquaintance prevailed upon him to face up to his duty. About the time Ambrose Plamondon received his call from Harry Askin, the Cunard agent was publishing his first bulletin.

To Broadway it was the torpedoing of Charles Frohman. Those of the theater all knew his crippled condition, and did not really see how he could save himself.

The stock market, which was in its closing minutes, still had plenty of time to sag alarmingly. To Wall Street this brought the war suddenly home.

Embarrassed Department of State officials in Washington had already been queried about the sinking by scores of newsmen, before the official cable from London tapped through at 3:30 P.M. False hopes raised by early reports of many or all passengers saved were dispelled when Ambassador Page advised:

The *Lusitania* was torpedoed off the Irish Coast and sunk in half an hour. No news yet of passengers.

Reporters were met at the German Embassy with a half-suppressed dread. A counselor, Prince Von Hatzfeldt Trachenberg, took the first onslaught, while Count von Bernstorff collected his quota of wits and waited further instruction from Berlin.

"They did not want to kill anybody," the Prince asserted. Many reporters filed it away as an imperishable gem.

Former President Teddy Roosevelt denounced the action as "piracy on a vaster scale of murder than any oldtime pirate ever practiced." Now it occurred to him that his Rough Riders would mount horses again, and he thundered, "It seems inconceivable that we can refrain from taking action . . . we owe it to humanity . . . to our own national self-respect!"

At the White House President Wilson was reported as being "deliberate and calm."

In Taftville, Connecticut, Bill Smith had finished his shift, and was relaxing at home. His shirt sleeves were rolled up and he was wondering if it would be a rainy week end—too rainy possibly for fishing—when George Weller, who ran the newspaper and candy store, appeared at his screened front door.

"They got the *Lusitania*, Bill," he said.

Bill was not really surprised that his mother-in-law's ship had been sunk. But he felt that she was alive.

"Well, she was told not to sail," he replied, "but you know how it is. Some people have to learn the hard way."

Deep inside he did not really believe that a torpedo, or even perhaps two torpedoes, would be enough to stop the durable and determined Elizabeth Duckworth.

As Bill Smith scratched his head and continued making small talk with George Weller, East Coast afternoon newspapers were already rolling off the presses. As they had done once before during the year, when the European war broke out in August, editors dusted off what they profanely called "second coming" type—inches high, the letters looked to readers.

All papers phrased it a little differently, but they spelled out the same stunning fact:

LUSITANIA TORPEDOED OFF IRELAND BY GERMAN SUBMARINE

In Boston, where the news was greeted with somewhat more restraint than elsewhere, there nevertheless was a rash of false information. The headlines included:

REMAINED AFLOAT 12 HOURS

Mrs. Lauriat, the mother of the Boston bookseller, admitted that she had felt "terrible that my son insisted on going." She was optimistic, however, pointing out that "in most cases of this sort, they have either been taken off by the Germans before the ship is torpedoed, or else have had time for rescue."

In the Boston Cunard office, ticket agents were startled to see Edward Bowen walk in. There had been some confusion in the last-minute cancellation of the wealthy shoe dealer's passage, and they thought he was aboard the *Lusitania*. He took a certain pleasure in assuring them he was not, but asked for accommodations on the *Ordina*, scheduled to sail within the week.

Flags were half-masted in East Aurora, New York, and pictures of Elbert Hubbard were draped in black crepe in store windows. Shocked, sorrowing Roycrofters, almost unable to continue their day's work, listened to young Bert's assurances:

"My father's not dead, nor Alice Hubbard. The news they are is false. They must have been saved."

Then he called a newspaper friend in New York, Arthur Brisbane, to inquire what he knew about the reports.

The switchboard at the telephone exchange of East Aurora was flooded with calls way out of proportion to the size of the hamlet. Operator Emma Yaggie worked far into the night, switching in the plugs for calls from exchanges as far away as California and even Mexico.

Premonitions belatedly came to light all over the country. Twenty miles north of East Aurora, in Buffalo, Mrs. William H. Brown mentioned one of them: her husband had had a dream the night before he sailed on the *Lusitania*. In the dream the liner was torpedoed and he himself was lost.

The Pittsburgh area had given its quota of citizens to the *Lusitania*—some twenty passengers in all. In nearby Ellwood City, friends were concerned about the Alfred Smiths, their infant Bessie and their six-year-old daughter Helen. Little Helen, they recalled, had spoken excitedly many times in the past few weeks of her impending visit to her grandparents in Liverpool.

And Herbert Owens, also of Ellwood City, went home early from the steel mill, sick and almost speechless with dread. His wife and two little sons, Ronald and Reginald, were on the *Lusitania*.

A Pittsburgh chemist claimed that 250,000 pounds of tetrachloride, from his laboratory, were aboard the *Lusitania*. He said the deadly stuff was manifested as "8 packages of drugs" and added blandly that it was intended for use in poison-gas bombs.

Nobody took him very seriously.

In Chicago, Ambrose Plamondon's sisters, Marie and Charlotte, received the first news in an abrupt way. They were

talking on the telephone when the operator, perhaps inad-
vertently, switched a newspaper reporter onto the line.

"Do you have any comment on the possible loss of your
mother and father in the sinking of the *Lusitania?*" he asked
bluntly.

Neither was the hysterical type and they went right to work
to try to find out. They contacted an uncle, Dr. John B.
Murphy. He sent a cable off to the Guinness Company in
Dublin and to the London offices of the Swift Company. The
Swifts had been close friends of the Plamondons.

Another friend, Mrs. Roger Sullivan, said she was related
to the Kinsale wireless operator and also knew the parish
priest at Clonakilty. She lost no time in framing a message
to them.

For Marie and Charlotte the afternoon quickly worked
into a fever pitch. The telephone rang constantly in their
comfortable gray stone house, and people were calling at the
door all day. They paid little attention to the rising wind
off Lake Michigan, did not notice the increasing sway to the
trees framed in their big square parlor window, as a stormy
spring evening brewed.

Reporters in Chicago were intrigued with another family.
William Mounsey, a local expressman, was rushing to Liverpool on the *Lusitania,* accompanied by his daughter and son-
in-law, Mr. and Mrs. C. L. Lund. His mission was a bizarre
one. His wife had been missing since the preceding year from
the sinking of the *Empress of Ireland* in the St. Lawrence;
now there was word from Liverpool that a woman, half out
of her mind in an institution, kept babbling about a terrible
dread of the water while claiming her name was Mounsey.

In South Bend, Indiana, where Father Basil Maturin was

widely read and respected, priests hastened into the chapel
to pray. Some recalled a passage from one of his books:

> It was a great victory of the human mind which annihilated
> space and time, and circled the globe with telegraph wires.
> But greater still is the victory which gives a man strength and
> courage to receive with equanimity over those wires a message
> telling him that all he valued in life has been taken from him.

Maude Adams, appearing at the Grand Theater, in Kansas
City, weepingly denied she was ever married to Charles Frohman, as some had believed her to be. The audience noted her
face was tear-streaked, her voice on the thin edge of cracking
when she commenced her next performance of *Quality Street*.

In San Francisco a pall was cast over the gaiety of the Exposition.

In Victoria, B.C., mobs were galvanized early into action.
The *Deutsches Verein,* or German Club, was wrecked: windows smashed, furniture dragged into the street and axed.
The proprietors fled as pipe-wielding men paused to hang a
picture of King George over the bar, then helped themselves
to the liquor. Violence spread to a brewery, to a German
hotel, to other establishments, until finally martial law was
proclaimed and troops rushed in from Vancouver.

The entire Dominion staggered under the news. From the
Pacific coast across to Newfoundland, scatterings of her sons
and daughters were aboard the lost ship: soldiers, men en
route to enlist in the armed forces, others well known profes-
sionally or in society.

It seemed to Montrealers as if the lights had suddenly gone
out. Everyone knew or had seen pictures of Lady Marguerite
Allan and her beautiful thirteen-year-old twin daughters,
Anna and Gwen, often seen riding in their pony gig. They

had sailed on the *Lusitania* to be reunited with the rest of
the family.

Newspapermen in large cities and tiny towns alike were
digging into their morgues to find out more about this wondrous ship which now lay at the bottom of the Atlantic approaches to the Irish Sea. They exhumed long, rhapsodic
articles like that in the *Scientific American* of August, 1907:

> The double bottom covering the whole of the ship's length
> is 5 feet in depth . . . There are nine decks in all, and the
> hull is divided into 175 separate watertight compartments
> which surely establishes the claim that she is unsinkable by
> any ordinary disaster.

The Boston *Globe* recalled an official statement at the time
of the *Titanic* disaster: "a similar accident to the *Lusitania*
would have left the ship afloat and able to proceed under her
own steam."

These read like epitaphs to editors as they searched further
to find ways to illustrate the ship's vastness. They discovered,
for example, the *Lusitania* was thirty-four feet longer than
the Capitol building in Washington, and hastened with the
help of artists to superimpose a photograph of her against
the Capitol. Other editors up-ended the vessel beside the
Woolworth building.

The same thing was being done on Fleet Street, in London,
but the backgrounds used for comparison were London
Bridge, Parliament House, and the Lord Nelson column in
Trafalgar Square.

The photo editor of the *Daily News* went even further.
His touch-up men took a funnel of the *Lusitania* and put it
in the middle of Argyle Street, Glasgow, where the breadth
visibly stretched from sidewalk to sidewalk. Still not satisfied,

he had trams and cabs rolling through its cavernous interior.

Late afternoon extras were on the street in record time. Though Londoners were already used to the daily carnage at Gallipoli and Ypres and constantly fearful of the new Zeppelin menace, news of the torpedoing came as a shock. Incredulous London bobbies even stopped newsboys and threatened to take them to the police station—until they read the article themselves and realized, unhappily, that the news was true.

Slowly, the lobby of the Cunard office in Cockspur Street began to fill with people, for the most part quiet and restrained. Two middle-aged ladies, for example, sat to one side "splendidly hoping against hope."

Winston Churchill, First Lord of the Admiralty, already had an explanation. He asserted, defensively, that "our resources do not enable us to provide destroyer escorts for mail and passenger ships . . . the general principle is that merchant traffic must look after itself."

Ambassador Walter Hines Page, at his Grosvenor Square offices, had received a flash at four o'clock that the *Lusitania* had been torpedoed but that the liner had been beached and all souls saved. A friend at Lloyd's advised him that the ship had been blown up by an "infernal machine" hidden aboard. In not very many more minutes the sixty-year-old North Carolinan was handed another message from Consul Frost which proved how optimistic had been the first telegram.

By the time he crossed Grosvenor Square to his residence at No. 6 the American Ambassador to England was lost in "dumb stupefaction." He would have to go through with his dinner party that night—but he knew he would be interrupted all evening as the grim bulletins kept flowing over from the Embassy's code room.

Even Englishmen fighting in France heard the news before the day was out. E. J. Flower, of Wiltshire, surrounded by cables in a telephone pit outside of Ypres, saw one of the signalmen lift off an earphone as he turned to a buddy.

"Say, mates—the *Lusitania*'s been sunk," he announced. "Just came over the wires from headquarters."

"Was she torpedoed?" asked another soldier whom Flower took for "a country bumpkin."

"Naw, you bloody fool," said the signalman, replacing his headset, "ran agin' a shrimp!"

In the telephone control pit outside Ypres, the evening of May 7, 1915, they thought that was awfully funny. The shells burst overhead and their own very real war continued on.

In a suburb of Liverpool the news was brought to Captain Turner's mother by a close friend of the family. Mrs. Turner was a distinguished-looking and gentle old lady, with finely chiseled features and snow-white hair which hung in long curls. No one knew the list of the survivors at that point.

"I am deeply distressed at the loss of so much life as there surely is and of so fine a ship," she said calmly, "but let me assure you that Will most surely will come through. I know that he will do his duty to the end, but I also know he will not drown."

There was a milling crowd about the Cunard office in Liverpool far greater and less composed than that in London. Lorrie Dolphin, a nurse and the aunt of little Avis, was busily giving professional aid to the hysterical as she herself waited anxiously the long day and night for the first survivor lists.

In the big home port of the *Lusitania* there was wild despair throughout hundreds of homes. Liverpool had given most heavily to the *Lusitania:* crewmen, officers, stewards, and stewardesses. By evening gangs of irate men, women beside them, were roaming the drab, coal-smelling city systematically smashing in windows of any shop bearing a German name—or a name which sounded remotely Teutonic. The many German pork butcher shops were a favorite target.

Police bobbies, as the destruction continued, remained undecided as to which of three possible courses of action to pursue: arrest the mob, watch dispassionately, or cheer.

It was a day of understatement and the London *Times* itself was not to be left out, chronicling, "there had been considerable display of feeling in Liverpool."

News was slow in reaching the tiny isle of Foula, or "Ultima Thule," far to the north off the Scottish coast. Even when it did, neighbors were loath to tell the lady at the "Hace." Mrs. Holbourn was on the stone steps leading to the garden when the bell pealed at her garden gate and an impetuous friend blurted:

"The *Lusitania*'s down!"

The wife of the professor, faint, clutched onto the door till her household staff hurried to her. When fully revived by some brandy, she surprised her servants and a gathering knot of neighbors by announcing that she knew "Bernard" was safe—she had a vision last night, she confided, in which she foresaw the disaster. She had also seen very plainly the "King" of Foula come safely to shore.

In Wales, headline posters were rushed onto the street before editors took time for a second look. By late evening a classic had been produced:

GREAT NATIONAL DISASTER
D. A. THOMAS SAVED

Friends of the Welsh coal mine magnate, chuckling in their clubs, resolved to obtain one of the posters to present to Thomas and his daughter, Lady Mackworth, when they finally arrived home.

CHAPTER 15

The tank steamer *Narragansett* had covered almost twenty-two miles and was within thirteen miles of the *Lusitania*'s last radioed position when, at 3:45 P.M., Second Officer John Letts sighted a periscope off the port quarter.

"Periscope!" he shouted across the bridge to Captain Harwood. The cry was picked up and passed from man to man, from bow to stern, and below decks to the engine room.

A torpedo streaked toward the ship before the helm could be put over. Those on the bridge watched it nearing them. The sun still shone, the waters were calm and blue—it made this monstrous thing all the more unbelievable.

Feet away, it passed astern of the *Narragansett* and vanished to starboard toward the shore. At the same time the periscope disappeared.

Captain Harwood looked at Letts, and Letts looked at the helmsman. The helmsman looked over his shoulder at the quartermaster behind him. The quartermaster's knuckles were white as he started to write the notation in his log.

Just about this time, allowing for the difference in clock settings, Kapitan Schwieger had fired another torpedo, which he indicated was his last. It "fouled" astern of his target, which he took to be a Cunard freighter. He indicated in his log that the missile was defective.

His position was somewhere between Kinsale and Fastnet and now he was homeward bound. He set course to the Orkneys again; he would return through the North Sea mine barrage, threading his way toward Wilhelmshaven, instead of Emden, to be outfitted for his next patrol.

It did not take Captain Harwood long to reach a new conclusion. All seemed clear now. The SOS he had received an hour and a half before was a decoy, flashed by the Germans.

"Starboard helm!" he commanded the helmsman.

Slowly, the bow swung westward, away from Ireland. The crew watched the curving, frothing wake with relieved hearts. For the next hour the ship followed a zigzag course, away from the *Lusitania*.

About 5:00 P.M. the *Etonian* overhauled the *City of Exeter*. Captain Wood, of the former ship, estimated he was now only a few miles from the *Lusitania*. As the *City of Exeter* crossed the bows of the Leyland Liner, Captain Wood had the quartermaster signal with his alphabet flags:

"Have you heard anything of the disaster?"

Before Captain Rae of the *City of Exeter* could reply in semaphone "wigwag" language, Wood sighted the periscope of a submarine which somehow had maneuvered between the two ships, about a quarter of a mile distant and directly ahead of his *Etonian*.

Then the submarine dived, with a splash that was visible to those on lookout aboard the *Etonian*. Wood signaled the engine room for "every available inch of speed," and was gratified at the "prompt response."

In a few minutes Wood saw the periscope reappear astern.

The submarine followed the ship, but kept dropping slowly behind. Wood estimated the U-boat's speed to be about two knots slower than that of the *Etonian*.

When there was a more comfortable gap between the submarine and the *Etonian*, Captain Wood spotted another U-boat, riding on the surface off the starboard bow. He swung away from it. The submarine followed.

In about eight minutes the *Etonian*'s pursuer submerged. The periscope of the first one had now vanished astern. But both steamers, the *Etonian* and *City of Exeter*, continued to race westward, seeking to put as much water between themselves and the U-boats as possible. It was up to the Navy, their captains reasoned, to come to the aid of the *Lusitania*.

The *Etonian* and *City of Exeter* were in all probability much closer to the spot where the *Lusitania* had sunk than the officers on either realized, for two steamers, probably the *Etonian* and the *City of Exeter*, were sighted by several lifeboats.

One of these lifeboats was "commanded" by Elizabeth Duckworth and the three men, who had succeeded in pulling about forty persons out of the water. Elizabeth and the men, exhausted from rowing, believed the two steamers were coming to their rescue. Then they watched the steamers change course and gradually get smaller on the horizon, leaving twin trails of coal smoke across the sky. Elizabeth reasoned, "They evidently know nothing of our predicament."

Timmins and Rita Jolivet, elsewhere, also thought they saw them.

When Elizabeth arrived back at the trawler, *Peel 12*, the fishermen lined the rails and gave her and the three other heroes of the lifeboat "a rousing cheer." The survivors were transferred to the fishing smack, which remained becalmed.

Professor Holbourn's boat also arrived at the trawler, adding to its already-overcrowded condition. Holbourn assisted the women survivors into the cramped fish-reeking hold, and next the wet male passengers. He returned on deck and sat, shivering.

Finally, as the condition of many survivors grew worse, the tug *Stormcock* came alongside and took off the *Lusitania*'s passengers. The crew of the rescue vessel—a famous old craft which once had given tow to the cable-laying behemoth, *Great Eastern*—paused momentarily in their work to bring a couple on board from a much more precarious kind of float.

W. E. G. Jones, third electrician of the lost Cunarder, a man who never had swum in his life, had clung to wooden debris until he saw a large box floating toward him. It turned out to be one of the sturdy wooden lockers kept on deck for storage of lifebelts. He struggled aboard it, was surprised to find a lady already inside, sitting rather placidly, with water sloshing up to her waist.

"Is there room for one more?" he recalled asking. The two sat there, side by side, cold and wet, until they bobbed alongside of the *Stormcock*.

Holbourn noticed that the cabin stove of the tug was lacking a fire. To the lecturer this seemed "a further instance of folly."

"For God's sake, get it alight!" he told the captain. "There are people dying of pneumonia."

A blaze was kindled. Holbourn, however, had another tiff over the listing of names of survivors.

"There are agonized relatives and friends all eager to have news," he pleaded. But Holbourn could not prevail upon the captain.

Wiemann, who had thought help would never come, was

more satisfied with the reception aboard his rescue vessel. Tins of corned beef and a barrel of sailors' biscuits were broken out for "one of the nicest meals" he ever had.

Lady Mackworth was picked up at dusk by a rowboat and transferred to the steamer, *Bluebell*. She owed her salvation to something even less substantial than a lifebelt box—a wicker chair that had bobbed under her while she floated unconscious. It elevated her just high enough so that she could be distinguished in the fading light. Along with dead bodies, she was hauled aboard.

"I rather think there s some life in this woman," a midshipman mentioned as he lifted her onto the deck of the *Bluebell*. "You'd better try and see."

When she awoke it was dark. She was lying on deck and wrapped in blankets, surprised to find that otherwise she did not have on a stitch of clothing. As she revived, a sailor came by, looked at her, and said, "That's better."

He returned several times and repeated the same thing. It became faintly amusing.

She had the vague idea that "something had happened," but believed she was on the deck of the *Lusitania*, and could not understand why her own stewardess—instead of this strange sailor—was not tending her.

Finally the sailor brought a cup of lukewarm tea which hastened her memory back. She decided there was nothing seriously wrong, although her whole body continued to shake violently and her teeth were chattering "like castanets." A sharp pain in her back she attributed to rheumatism.

Now the sailor suggested she go below to warm herself, as he confessed:

"We left you up here to begin with as we thought you

were dead and it did not seem worthwhile cumbering up the cabin with you."

He contemplated with misgivings the prospect of transporting her down the cabin stairs. "It took three men to lift you on board. . . ."

Lady Margaret believed she could walk, tried it, and found it required three men once more. The third, this time, held back her long, dripping hair. She was placed on the captain's bunk, recently vacated by a survivor who had recovered.

Soon she and a large group in the heat and light of the cabin became "a little drunk" with the simple ecstasy of being alive. They talked and laughed loudly, until a sailor entered and asked if they had lost anyone in the sinking. It had a sudden, sobering effect, reminding her that she still did not know what had become of her father.

One woman, who had been laughing only seconds before, now concluded that her husband was drowned. "He is all I have in the world," she said.

Margaret Mackworth could imagine the rupture and then the long remaking of the woman's life. It depressed her, for the woman in her daze and shock had been "full of cheerfulness and laughter."

Later on she recognized Captain Turner. He sat in a corner of the cabin wrapped in a blanket, cold, exhausted, stunned by the magnitude of what had happened.

His gold braid had saved him. A sharp-eyed sailor on the *Bluebell* had seen its glint after he had been in the water more than three hours. A sailor, Jack Roper, had supported him for the final minutes of his ordeal.

Sitting near Turner, and equally silent, was young Officer Bestic, also saved by a uniform. In Bestic's case, however, it was the new uniform he wished to take off before going below to the baggage hold.

"Bissitt," as Turner persisted in calling him, arrived on board alive after being supported variously by an overturned boat, half-wrecked collapsibles, and air tanks.

Captain Turner was addressed by at least one passenger, a woman who had been sitting quietly in the outer cabin. In a gentle, dispassionate tone of voice, hollow and almost devoid of emotion, she accused him of a "lack of organization and discipline" on the *Lusitania*.

A little while before, with the same, almost frightening calm, she had told other survivors how she had been instructed to place her young son on a raft. She did so, and then the raft capsized. Her boy never came back to the surface.

"His death was unnecessary," she told Turner.

A sailor remarked that she must be hysterical. But Lady Margaret opined that the bereaved mother "appeared to be the one person on board who was not."

At evening Theodate Pope was discovered by the trawler *Julia*, almost down to its scuppers with survivors, as well as with those who did not survive. Theodate, kept afloat by an oar, was unconscious. Sailors fished her up with boat hooks and laid her on the deck among the dead.

An acquaintance of the voyage, Mrs. Theodore Naisch, of Kansas City, Missouri, recognized Theodate. She just had a hunch there might be a spark of life there, even though Theodate was stiff and cold from the salt water and felt to the other woman's touch "like a sack of cement."

Mrs. Naisch persuaded two sailors to give Miss Pope artificial respiration. They cut her clothing off with a carving knife and worked patiently for nearly two hours. Finally her

breathing became steady, although she remained semicon-
scious for another hour or two. They wrapped her in a
blanket and placed her on the floor before the charcoal fire
in the captain's cabin.

It was almost ten-thirty that night when Theodate became
aware of the small open-grate fire and a pair of gray-trousered
legs beside it. Turning her head, which still ached horribly
from the blow she had received in the water, she raised her
eyes and saw a man leaning over a table, looking at her.

"She's conscious," she heard him say. Two women patted
her and said the doctor was on his way.

Theodate asked the women their names, then realized
what an effort it was to talk. She was shaking violently despite the heat from the fire, had no idea where she was nor
any recollection of the shipwreck.

Theodate Pope was relatively lavished with finery to be
wrapped in a blanket. Avis Dolphin, for one, had been bun-
dled in a rug on her rescue vessel, before being placed close
to a stove.

By dusk the rescue fleet was out in force. They swarmed
over the waters beyond Kinsale like lobster boats dipping
among the rocks after sunrise to inspect their pots. The boats
almost defied description or an accurate count. There were
two or three longboats, with oarsmen, from the smallest fishing villages. And there were harbor ferries and trawlers ranging in size up to the relatively large Greek coaster, *Katarina*
—whose captain showed remarkable courage even in being
there—and ancient warships like the *Juno* which actually
picked up a few survivors before scurrying back to port.

Many of the *Lusitania*'s crew and passengers, including
Brooks' and Bernard's boatloads, were transferred to a creaking, picturesque craft, the *Flying Fish*. One of the last of the

side-wheelers, she was a tender in Queenstown for larger vessels which anchored in the harbor. Those who had walked her decks before affectionately called her the "Galloping Goose."

Of all reunions on board the "Galloping Goose," passengers agreed the most touching was that between Margaret Gwyer, still blackened from the funnel, and her minister-husband. At first, as she ran to him, he did not recognize her. When he did, however, he quickly clutched her and they stood there like two smudged, grotesque circus clowns, crying and laughing.

Bernard, in his wet, grimy clothes, paced the limited deck space to keep warm, and reflected on the number of naval auxiliaries that he now noticed racing about for "a belated rescue." D. A. Thomas was more bitter.

"Outrageous, simply outrageous!" he exploded. "The boats, the deplorable inefficiency, I mean. Did you see what was happening? The standard of human efficiency is far below what we are entitled to expect. Today it was ghastly."

Bernard, thinking that Thomas ought to be "a field marshal or an admiral" replied: "It's got to start at the top—can't expect efficiency from the crew if you don't set an example on the bridge."

Many survivors, who had never found even the shaky haven of a collapsible, were plucked directly out of the waters, now colder with evening. Some middle-aged men and women, like Theodate Pope, were miraculously alive after being immersed for four or even seven hours. They were pulled off oars, planking boxes, and kegs. R. H. Duncan, first senior third engineer, and a lady were found at dusk clinging to a small air tank. The woman had clutched her dead baby for the first two hours until Duncan prevailed upon her to set the lifeless body adrift.

The Reverend H. M. Simpson, of British Columbia, minus clerical collar and coat, had pulled an oar of his collapsible like one inspired, pausing only to assist survivors out of the water. One of them was a most durable little boy—Bobbie Kay, of New York, who was flushed with measles that had broken out during the crossing. His mother, Mrs. James Kay, had been washed away before his eyes.

The Reverend Simpson finally attracted attention to his waterborne flock by waving a pair of trousers on an oar.

Robert Leith, Marconi man, was hoisted out of a half-submerged boat, alive. So was Martin Mannion, who had paused for a final drink all by himself in Second Class smoking saloon. He couldn't remember for the life of him how he got from the saloon to the deck, into the water, or even into the boat.

Grace French, acquaintance of Archie Donald, saved her life in macabre fashion. She kept afloat atop the corpse of some large man.

Another woman was picked up at sunset from the glint of her large diamond ring. Her hand was floating flush with the water but her head was beneath the waves. Sailors on the fishing vessel that had spotted her tried artificial respiration —in vain.

Kessler, his busy black beard sodden and salt-caked, was one of three survivors from one collapsible. It had sprung a leak and foundered until it was awash, then bobbed to the surface again. Originally there had been some fifty men and women in it. After at least seven swampings the number had dwindled to the three who somehow mustered strength to swim back each time.

Minute by minute now the living and the dead were coming aboard the rescue fleet—men and women of all classes of the *Lusitania,* all financial and social gradations: C. T. Jeffrey, Robert Timmins, Dr. Houghton, Ernest Cowper, Dr. Fisher, who had been nearly four hours in the water, Rita Jolivet, Dorothy Conner, Florence Padley, Virginia Bruce Loney, Kathleen Kaye, Edith Williams, the oldest of the six Williams children from Plainfield, New Jersey, also her brother Eddie . . . In no boat, nor in the water now being cloaked with darkness, had anyone seen her mother, or her four brothers and sisters . . . nor had anyone helped aboard even one member of the Crompton family of eight, from quiet St. Martin's Lane, Philadelphia.

And where were Mr. Vanderbilt, Producer Frohman, Sage Hubbard and Alice, novelist Forman, Marie de Page, explorer Stackhouse, shipbuilder Hopkins, genealogist Withington, art curator Lane, and distiller Campbell, who had labeled submarine talk "a lot of tommyrot"? Where, indeed, were they?

Lady Allan, from Montreal, was in one of the rescue boats. With Lady Allan were her two maids, Emily Davis and Annie Walker. But where were her beautiful twin daughters? Lady Marguerite had held hands with them when they jumped from the *Lusitania,* saying that they would die together.

Where was Theodate Pope's maid, Emily Robinson—not so lucky or vigorous perhaps as Lady Allan's? At least Emily Robinson's name had been recorded, as had that of Frohman's valet, William Staunton. Other maids and valets had disappeared, with only the anonymous epitaph, "Mrs. Smith's maid," or "Mr. Jones' valet."

Where was Walter Scott Quarrie, young ventilating engineer from the Isle of Man, on his first voyage? Where was

Father Basil Maturin? Or Minister Loynd? Where was Purser McCubbin, or Staff Captain Anderson, last seen running aft in his shirt sleeves? Where was INS photographer Patrick Jones, with his "greatest pictures ever"?

And Chief Officer Piper, who was running forward to close the fo'csle "scuttle" doors, one last frantic gamble to buy a little more time for the fast-sinking ship and its passengers? Where was Piper, whom fellow crew members already were thinking of as a hero?

A strange note of rivalry soon entered the rescue operations. The *Stormcock,* loaded with almost as many dead as living, was headed for land as it met two Arklow fishing vessels, the *Daniel O'Connell* and the *Elizabeth,* out of Kinsale. The two, equipped with the extravagance of auxiliary power, had already picked up survivors.

The *Stormcock* hove to alongside the two smaller craft, and the captain asked for their passengers to be transferred to the *Stormcock.* Already the Irish coastal villages were vying for the honor of rescue. An argument ensued.

The two Kinsale skippers, Jimmy Hagen of the *O'Connell,* and White of the *Elizabeth,* protested that the *Stormcock* was big enough to continue her job a bit longer before putting back to Queenstown. White pointed out that he should hurry his passengers to Kinsale, which was closer than Queenstown, since a few of the women were "in a very bad way."

The *Stormcock* won out and took the other survivors aboard. Some died before reaching Queenstown. Doctors later declared that shock and immersion probably would have claimed these victims even if they had been rushed to Kinsale. But that did not allay hurt, local feelings. Passions in Kinsale against neighboring Queenstown and its vessels ran high.

Sunset was well past, and the harbor waters off Queenstown were a dark mirror as the hodgepodge rescue fleet began to arrive. The small vessels glided swiftly past the shadowy shapes of the Royal Dock Yard and the Royal Yacht Club. There was a vague aroma of food and peat fires.

But the safety of port was anticlimactic to the survivors; they had struggled too hard for this moment, and their capacity for emotion was exhausted.

People like Herbert Ehrhardt, Archie Donald, and Miss Winter were busy tending to others in more desperate condition as the vessels neared the quays. Ehrhardt, the student from Toronto, had not quite abandoned hope for resuscitating the woman they had fished out of the water, apparently dead.

The *Flying Fish* stood offshore for what seemed to her passengers like hours while her bridge blinked back and forth for permission to berth in a slip she did not generally use. It appeared to Bernard, for one, that the red tape they encountered, in harbor traffic and customs, displayed the "magnificent unconcern" of the shore officials.

As tiny skiffs swarmed alongside, survivors obtained the impression that no one was particularly surprised that the *Lusitania* had been sunk. An old man in a rowboat remarked, matter-of-factly, "She's been waitin' for ye for days." Other remarks revealed that submarines had been sighted in bays like Glandore, Dunmanus, and Dingle with a regularity that hinted at their always having been there.

When finally the *Julia* came alongside, a doctor stepped aboard. He examined Theodate Pope in the captain's cabin, then called two sailors to assist her ashore. They made a chair out of their locked hands. Failing to hold onto their shoulders as they lifted her, she almost fell over backward.

The doctor came up behind them and steadied her as they started toward the gangplank.

"Way, way!" one of the sailors shouted at the curious Queenstown citizens.

The captain of the *Bluebell* asked Margaret Mackworth if she was ready to disembark. Seized with a sudden modesty, she protested she had only her "tiny" blanket for covering, but might manage with a couple of safety pins. This brought "hoots of laughter" from the sailors. Someone produced a "British warm" soldier's greatcoat. Wearing this and the captain's carpet slippers, she started up the gangway. The task was more than she had anticipated.

"I must have been pretty weak," she recalled, "for I had to get down on my hands and knees and crawl onto it. At the other end of the gangway my father was waiting."

Captain Turner, still wrapped in a blanket like some solemn, aging Indian chieftain, was recognized as he padded off. A restrained chorus of cheers arose from the Irish townspeople.

Olive North, from the mine sweeper *Brock,* watched a male survivor leap onto the wooden barrier at the gangway of the pier. Shouting hysterically, he seemed to think he was back on the *Lusitania.* Two policemen finally pulled him down.

Consul Frost waited at the strangely hushed wharves. Appalled by what he saw, Frost reported:

We saw the ghastly procession of these rescue ships as they landed the living and the dead that night under the flaring gas torches along the Queenstown waterfront. The arrivals began soon after eight o'clock and continued at close intervals until about eleven o'clock. Ship after ship would come up out of the darkness and sometimes two or three could be just described awaiting their turns in the cloudy night to discharge bruised and shuddering women, crippled and half-clothed men and a few wide-eyed little children. . . . Women caught at our sleeves and begged desperately for word of their husbands, and men with choking efforts of matter-of-factness moved ceaselessly from group to group, seeking a lost daughter or sister or even bride. Piles of corpses like cordwood began to appear among the paint kegs and coils of rope on the shadowy old wharves. Every voice in that great mixed assemblage was pitched in unconscious undertones, broken now and then by painful coughing fits or suppressed hysteria. . . .

The *Lusitania* was in.

CHAPTER 16

Queenstown was turned into a "vast charnel house." Its normal tenor was disrupted as though a major battle had been fought on its outskirts.

Some of the survivors, already resuming their lives, went off in search of lodging. Others had already been assigned accommodations by harassed Cunard representatives. The Queens Hotel, with its forty-three rooms the largest in town, speedily became the landbound equivalent of First Class aboard the *Lusitania*. Its owner, of German extraction, fled to the basement, where he locked himself in among the wine barrels.

Other hotels became more of a cosmopolitan melting pot. In the Rob Roy, for example, Wiemann shared a room with C. T. Hill, one of the men whose table he had served in First Class dining saloon. They had a good laugh over the case of Hill's treasured apple cider, part of which he had donated to the waiter.

"The fishes are drinking it now," Wiemann philosophized.

Dorothy Conner found herself asking matter-of-factly for "room and bath," just as she would upon arriving in any

American city. The clerk showed no special reaction as he
called out her number and told her to move on. She was assigned to a room with five other women.

Dorothy asked for a hot bath and toddy. After what seemed
hours she was presented with a small bowl of tepid water and
a bottle of cold lemon soda. The elderly woman who brought
it delivered, as a bonus, a lecture on selfishness.

James Brooks, a teetotaler, was also thirsty. He ordered a
fifth of Irish whisky. Then, with Charles Jeffrey, his roommate, he finished off the bottle. It coated life with a pleasant
glaze. The two did not even think to look twice at the procession of scantily clad women moving past their half-opened
door. Nor, at one stage of the early morning, did it surprise
Brooks to hear Jeffrey ask a virtually naked young lady, wash-
ing coal dust and grime from herself across the hall, if he
could get anything for her in town.

When she answered, "No, thank you," without looking up,
they accepted her response as natural.

Many, like Theodate Pope, were assisted to bed. She shivered violently in spite of large doses of brandy. In the lobby,
on her way up, Theodate had encountered the young man
who had never eaten his ice cream at lunch after all. He was
clad in a pink dressing gown, and was unable to answer her
pressing inquiries as to whether or not Edwin Friend had
been saved.

There was little rest that night for Theodate or anyone
else from the *Lusitania*. Men kept snapping on lights in
order to identify little children, obtain survivors' names, and
deliver or accept telegrams.

Avis Dolphin was tucked into bed and given a glass of hot
milk.

Archie Donald saw that Lorna Pavey and Miss Winter were registered at the Queens, then went, with Wilson and Bilbrough, in search of missing shipboard acquaintances.

Captain Turner was a guest in the apartment of a banker. He drank more tea, managed to dry his uniform, and appeared shortly on the streets. Those who recognized him thought he looked "fit."

Elizabeth Duckworth was given medical treatment for exposure and lodged in the Westbourne Hotel. Only then did she feel the effects of the long ordeal. For a woman of fifty-two, she had assumed too active a role. As she recalled it, she "broke down"—and was not to fully recover for many months. She also met Arthur Scott, the little boy she had helped into a lifeboat, and learned that a missionary was taking him to his home in Nelson, England.

Oliver Bernard was smitten with the nightmarish quality of the night and its macabre scenes. He roamed the city until well past daybreak, drawn by a terrible fascination into the morgues. There he saw, among other appalling sights, "a heap of what looked like battered, bruised, broken dolls laid aside as factory refuse might be." He could never forget the scene.

Nude, semi-nude, innocents, trophies of war, merely a number of babies so discoloured that it was difficult to believe that these effigies had ever lived. Mothers, wives and daughters lay in a row all round the shed, in sodden garments, not believably human persons of the day before. In the second shelter, sunlight filtering through grimy windows glinted on some gold braid that was little clue to the identity of one whose bloated features were smeared with bloody mucous; Staff Captain Anderson had stuck to his job, and had not drowned without a hard struggle. The third and last edition of this marine purgatory was heavy with evaporating moisture;

poor Charles Frohman alone was undisfigured; he must have died without protest before the sea could do its worst. . . .

. . . the most appalling impression this experience left . . . was that in death all human beings were alike, shapeless, inanimate clay; death masks of those victims would have revealed no individualities, nothing but a horrible, lifeless uniformity. What happened to all those images and likenesses of God?

Through the night and early morning Bernard encountered others looking for their families and friends, mothers seeking children, wives seeking husbands, husbands seeking wives, brothers seeking sisters, and children seeking parents. Soon, he was sure, he must encounter Bill Lindsey's little girl, Leslie, or her husband, Stewart Mason. He never did.

Yet Leslie was there. Consul Wesley Frost found her, on an embalmer's slab in an improvised operating room in the rear of the Cunard office. "She lay like a statue typifying assassinated innocence."

Stewart was washed ashore farther up the coast. The news was cabled to Lindsey in Boston. It "hung"—forever afterward—like a cerement over his big stone house next to the Charles River. It made the great hall, and the oaken staircase flaring upward on either side, from which Leslie had thrown her bride's bouquet days before, seem to Lindsey like a mausoleum.

By Saturday morning, when it was obvious that all had been landed who were going to be, signs appeared in the shop windows of Queenstown, and soon in other villages along the south Irish coast. Most read like this one:

Lusitania—missing baby: missing, a baby girl, 15 months old. Very fair curly hair and rosy complexion. In white woolen jersey and white woolen leggins. Tries to talk and walk. Name

Betty Bretherton. Please send any information to Miss Browne, Queens House, Queenstown.

Some survivors, happy to be alive, went shopping. Cunard had underwritten the clothing bill for those who were literally down to bare skin—and there were surprisingly many. In one dry goods shop, Beatrice Williams, who had been rescued by the *Bluebell,* recognized Captain Turner. He was wearing his full uniform except for his hat, which he was seeking to replace. It seemed to Beatrice, who was en route from Rock Island, Illinois, to her sick father in Wales, that Turner was creating an unnecessary fuss.

"You should be worrying about a hat," the young woman berated him, "when so many of us have lost everything we own. Why—you ought to be ashamed of yourself!"

A barrister from London, Webb Ware, arrived to press the search for Vanderbilt. He was empowered to charter tugs, organize parties to scour every inlet of the coast, to do anything in fact which might locate the wealthy playboy or his mortal remains. Ware posted a reward of 1000 dollars.

For finding bodies of less distinguished passengers, Cunard offered a reward of approximately five dollars.

A few of the missing were found. The Charles Plamondons, of Chicago, had been washed ashore. Mrs. Plamondon's pince-nez glasses were gone, her dress was still soot-stained despite its long immersion in the water.

When the news was cabled to the States, it came almost as a relief to Am in Furnald Hall and to his sisters in Chicago. Now the waiting and uncertainty were over. Mother and Dad were coming home. In mourning, Chicago half-masted many of its flags.

Pittsburgh, too, showed its bereavement. The steel town

had suffered heavily, with nine out of the twenty from that area gone. There, too, they had been proud to count their recent visitor, Marie de Page, an honorary citizen.

In Philadelphia it became increasingly certain all eight Cromptons, even their governess, Dorothy Allen, were lost. It staggered the neighbors on St. Martin's and Hartwell Lanes. Of the Hodges, only Dean, six, had been saved. William Hodges, the organist of Harper Memorial Church, his wife and son, Billy, Jr., were gone.

Hoboken mourned Mrs. Ogden Hammond. Her husband, a former ambassador, was safe. Mrs. Walter Mitchell, from Newark, was alive, but she had lost her husband and ten-month-old child.

James Brooks identified the body of Charles Klein from Connecticut. Because of the playwright's club foot, he could not mistake him. Nearby, he saw the body of a woman, still rigidly clutching a dead child in each arm.

Of Justus Miles Forman, far younger and stronger than his friends Klein or Frohman, there was not a trace. At the Hollis Street Theater in Boston, the curtain fell that night for the final time on his only play, *The Hyphen*.

In East Aurora the Roycrofters shops were empty and sealed like tombs. Life had come to a virtual halt, for the Sage was gone. "Bill Kaiser," some observed dourly, had won the last round after all.

Father Basil Maturin's body was borne over the pebbly shores of Ballycotton Bay by two old fishermen. In London's Brompton Oratory plans were set in motion for impressive last rites. This brought the flicker of a pious smile to those who had been closest to him, for the distinguished theologian had often predicted that his funeral would be held on a rainy day in some small, half-empty village church.

One body—that of Captain J. B. Miller, of Erie, Pennsylvania, of the U. S. Coast and Geodetic Survey—came ashore in Galway, 200 miles north.

The strongest survivors started along the coast afoot, searching for friends and dear ones. They poked in shallow inlets, asked questions of fishermen, old women, children, anyone they happened to see. Many swore they would circle the entire shoreline of Ireland before they would rest.

Mrs. Bilicke, wife of the man who had helped build Los Angeles, was among the searchers, seeking her husband.

Other survivors were fortunate enough to charter automobiles for their search, though the machines were ancient, steam-driven curiosities which proceeded with ominous uncertainty. Women held onto their hats and prayed anew.

Still others clopped slowly in horse carts along the back roads leading to the water, past the stone houses of the fisherfolk.

Herbert Ehrhardt, who had slept so soundly all night that a policeman recording names had had to shake him several times, found the mothers of two of the girls he had befriended. Both were quite ill and depressed. Ehrhardt searched all day without finding a trace of any of the children he had known. His role of Pied Piper had come to a sad conclusion, and he was sure he had lost his whole flock.

Yet, curiously enough, he happened to find his shoes—the ones he had given to a shivering passenger in the lifeboat. Trying to buy a new pair in a Queenstown shoe store, he saw his original pair discarded on the floor. Ehrhardt laced them on again and walked out.

Les Morton, the lookout, was searching the mortuaries for his brother, Cliff—at the same time Cliff was searching for him. The two met in this way and exchanged almost hysteri-

cal greetings of joy. They discovered that each had sent identical telegrams homes saying he was seeking the other. But
the nine others, who had jumped the *Naiad* in their impa-
tience to sail home, were lost.

There were semihumorous mixups that took a full day to
unravel: men and women of identical last names, but with
different mates, being at first quartered in the same rooms,
as the authorities assumed them to be husband and wife.

And everyone was glad to see that the *"Lusy's"* youngest
passenger, two-month-old Billy Doherty of Long Island, was
a survivor. So was his mother, Mrs. Millie Doherty. She posed
with him in her arms, smiling, for the photographers who
were congregating from all over the British Isles.

Alice Middleton, who had at first been mistaken for dead
by those who pulled her body from the water, regained full
consciousness at a Queenstown nursing home. Doctors agreed
that her recovery after a coma of some hours was indeed marvelous, and they dubbed her "Marvel." Alice believed she
had been saved by Vanderbilt's lifebelt. There was one
strange, disquieting aftermath—her hair was all falling out.
It was also happening to another survivor, Theodate Pope.

By Saturday afternoon the first boat trains left for Kings-
town and the Irish Sea ferry to Holyhead, just southwest of
Liverpool, to complete the journey interrupted by a torpedo.
The thought of even a ferryboat was too terrifying for some
survivors to contemplate, and they elected to tarry a while in
Ireland. Others, such as Wiemann, Hugh Johnston, and
crew survivors, were already awaiting passage to Liverpool.

In London, Sunday morning, Ambassador Page was up at
dawn to meet the first four trainloads, carrying eighty survivors, at Euston Station. Yet he held scant hope of finding
many fellow Americans in that group.

London was misty, quiet, smoky, as Page was driven to sooty old Euston, where he arrived at 6:00 A.M. The brooding quality of the sprawling old city somehow mirrored the profound depression of the American ambassador. Even the tooting, bustling railroad station seemed to possess a muted, mourning quality. Vendors stood hushed beside their tea carts and newspaper-magazine wagons.

When the first trainload rolled in from Holyhead, those who had been waiting since four and five that morning moved swiftly forward along the platform. One woman almost overcome with emotion, was overheard repeating the name, "Alexander Campbell."

The survivors were a ragged, sleepwalking lot, dazed, with "lustreless" eyes. They wore their makeshift, ill-fitting clothing purchased in the stores of Queenstown. A few carried their arms in slings, others had to be supported by their families or acquaintances of the voyage.

Some still slept inside the cars, but the attendants read out their names. The announcement of one name caused an outburst of joy from a man on the platform. He leaped an iron gate and conveyed the news excitedly to a group of ladies waiting in the concourse.

But their joy was short-lived as the attendant hurried over to them. He was sorry: the name should have been crossed off his list.

A mother recognized her ten-year-old boy and rushed to greet him. She clutched him and sobbed with hysterical relief.

A twelve-year-old boy, less fortunate, was led off to the Cunard office. He had been orphaned, as had Virginia Bruce Loney, by the sinking.

In the background several persons asked about Hugh

Lane. But no one seemed to know a thing about him, even whether he had survived.

A middle-aged man in black, accompanied by an army officer, arrived from the Cunard office where he had sat up the night. He went around asking questions of survivors as the trains pulled in. Finally, after the arrival of the fourth and last train that Sunday morning, he broke down and sobbed uncontrolledly.

Railroad officials and newspaper reporters observed one or two other men crying. It was an unaccustomed, unbelievable, and altogether terrible sight.

Dr. Antoine de Page had hurried across the English Channel from his hospital at La Panne. He was expecting Dr. Houghton—but had all but abandoned hope for his wife.

By midmorning Ambassador Page sadly walked away from the station platform. His eyes were hollow, he shuffled listlessly, looking in worse shape even than some of the injured survivors. As he passed, the rest of the crowd dispersed.

The next day, Monday, dawned warm and bright throughout the British Isles. In Queenstown people were awakened by the sound of horse carts moving over cobblestones. They looked out windows to see a procession of carts, each drawing one or two coffins draped with the Union Jack. There were not enough hearses, so wagons and horses had been gathered from all over County Cork for this funeral day.

All morning they passed, sometimes accompanied by military bands playing the doleful strains of Chopin's "Funeral March." Men and women stood hatless on the sidewalks, while flags throughout the city and on vessels in the harbor were at half-mast. Many residents shuttered their windows as a mark of respect.

It was a strange sight, the seemingly unending line of rustic, worn little carts, the swayed, plodding horses, the dirge of hoofbeats. Slowly the procession passed the familiar shops and pubs of a city known for lightheartedness, past The Anchor Bar, past Joseph Grogan's, and Tyler's, Ltd.

The carts rumbled through Queenstown, up past St. Colman's Cathedral, situated on the city's highest point, as the church bells tolled. They proceeded two miles out to the Old Church Cemetery. There soldiers had dug mass graves to receive this first large group of more than a hundred coffins bearing unidentified victims.

Just before the joint Protestant-Catholic services started at 4:00 P.M., a woman stepped forward and asked that a certain coffin be opened. An attendant obliged and she peered inside. Then she shook her head, turned, and walked away from the Old Church Cemetery.

By four-thirty the rites were over and the spectators moved slowly away. The strains of "Abide with Me" continued to ring in their ears—a hymn many of them would always associate with that sunny Irish afternoon, when wooden boxes, row upon row, were lowered into the ground, to be covered with earth and rock.

Even as the holy water had flashed in the sun "like a thin silver breath," as a reporter wrote, and incense smoke "mingled in the heavy air," Pope Benedict was telegraphing the Kaiser from Rome, "deploring his inhuman methods."

And Dr. De Page, in Queenstown, had identified the body of Marie. She would be buried in the Belgium she loved.

Sarah Lund, from Chicago, had finally arrived in Liverpool and looked at the woman in the nursing home allegedly off the *Empress of Ireland*. It was not her mother. And it was doubly tragic since Sarah's father, William Mounsey, and her

own husband as well had been lost as a result of this hopeless mission.

At Kinsale, J. J. Horgan, lawyer and coroner, was finishing up an inquest he had opened on Saturday. It was held in
the picturesque Market House, dating back centuries, before
a jury of twelve shopkeepers and fishermen, whom Horgan
considered "humble, honest citizens." It concerned the deaths
of the five victims whose bodies had been landed in Kinsale.

Two especially could not be forgotten. A Scottish girl,
Margaret McKenzie, who had previously moved to the
United States, had married James Shineman eleven days before the *Lusitania* sailed. Without telling her parents, they
embarked on this honeymoon voyage. They had been booked
originally on the *Cameronia*. A headstone in little St. Mul-
tose churchyard now marked the end of their lives.

Among the witnesses at the inquest was Captain Turner.
"Clad in a badly fitting old suit and still suffering from the
strain of his experience," according to one observer, "he
looked, and was, a broken man." At the end Horgan noticed
him "bowing his head [as] he burst into tears."

The spectacle of suffering and death at its shores had been
too much for the warm-hearted Irish, even with every reason
historically to favor the Germans over the English. At Horgan's direction the verdict was returned:

> That the deceased died from prolonged immersion and ex-
> haustion in the sea eight miles south south-west of the Old
> Head of Kinsale on Friday, 7th May, 1915, owing to the sink-
> ing of RMS *Lusitania* by torpedoes fired without warning
> by a German submarine. We find that this appalling crime
> was contrary to international law and the conventions of all
> civilized nations and we therefore charge the officers of the
> said submarine and the Emperor and Government of Germany

under whose orders they acted with the wilful and wholesale murder before the tribunal of the civilized world.

Meanwhile, the final casualties were being added up. Of the 1959 souls who had sailed aboard the *Lusitania,* 1198 had perished, including 785 passengers.

Of the 159 Americans, 124 had perished.

Of the 129 children, 94 perished. Included in the number of children were thirty-five infants, of whom all but four were lost.

The funerals had been held, other bodies would soon be shipped to home soil, and survivors were rapidly resuming life where it had been interrupted. The lists had been totaled.

Yet the books on the *Lusitania* were by no means closed.

CHAPTER 17

America was stunned, incredulous. Its own people —not even combatants—were suddenly war casualties.

Then shock gave way to a national anguish as the wave that had boiled up from the sinking *Lusitania* swept across the nation, arousing its citizens as they had not been aroused since Paul Revere. Anguish quickly was turned into a rising cry for action, which echoed and re-echoed in newspaper cartoons and editorials.

In New York the *Sun* depicted Kaiser Wilhelm fastening a medal around the neck of a mad dog, as a small flag labeled *Lusitania* disappeared under the waves. The Philadelphia *North American,* caricaturing Hohenzollern as a monster, had him drowning a woman with his own hands.

Rollin Kirby, in the *World,* visualized the same ruler sneering behind a black cloak while ghosts of children asked, "But Why Did You Kill Us?"

Denver's *Rocky Mountain News* declared, "Today humanity is aghast that such a thing . . . could be possible in the Twentieth Century." The Chicago *Tribune* counseled deliberation and urged Wilson be accorded the nation's back-

228

ing. The San Francisco *Chronicle* suggested a reappraisal of the nation's defenses, pointing out that the U-boat had relegated the dreadnought to the status of "junk."

On the other side of the Atlantic, the German press seemed to find the disaster a signal for rejoicing.

The Frankfurter *Zeitung* pronounced the torpedoing "an extraordinary success," and in Munich a medal was struck in commemoration. One side of it depicted passengers at a Cunard office buying tickets from a death's head, under the slogan, in German, "Business as Usual!" The other side showed the *Lusitania* sinking, its decks crammed with a fantastic cargo of airplanes and cannon, beneath the inscription, "No Contraband Goods!"

The medal, along with postcards in similar vein, found its way to Britain, France, and other countries of the Entente. The most puzzling thing was the clearly engraved date, "5 May."

In Philadelphia, President Wilson declared there was such a thing as being "too proud to fight," that a nation could be "so right" it need not "convince others by force." Not everyone agreed.

Six days after he sent the *Lusitania* to the bottom, Kapitanleutnant Schwieger nosed his *U-20* into Wilhelmshaven. He noted:

> The pilot who was taken along, Helmsman Lanz, of the reserve, has again done his duty very satisfactorily and was of great assistance in the enterprise since he knows all English ships by their build and can also tell at once at what speed they generally run.

It seemed an odd entry for the U-boat skipper who had already logged that he did not recognize the identity of his largest victim until he saw the gold letters on her bow, just before her death plunge. Nor did Schwieger meet with the acclaim he might have expected. Word filtered through Flotilla headquarters that the Kaiser was far from pleased now that he had had a chance to assess the world's reaction.

On May 13, also, the first "Wilson note" was dispatched to Germany. It asked her to disavow such acts as the sinking of the *Lusitania* and to give assurance against future attacks on unarmed merchant ships without warning.

Its assertion of America's "indisputable" rights was received with general satisfaction. Some, however, like former President Roosevelt, complained it was too mild; while Secretary of State Bryan thought it far too strong. Colonel Ed House, special adviser to Wilson, noted in his diary that "war with Germany is inevitable."

He recalled a noontime appointment with King George at Buckingham Palace on May 7, certainly not much more than two hours before the great Cunarder had been torpedoed.

"We fell to talking, strangely enough," House had noted that day, "of the probability of Germany sinking a transatlantic liner. He said, 'Suppose they should sink the *Lusitania* with American passengers on board.' "

House had thought it a curious remark, and he had decided to discuss it that evening when he would be guest of honor at the American Embassy. He wondered if Ambassador Page would agree with his reply to the king, which was to the effect that he thought America would be outraged enough, in such an eventuality, to enter the war.

Many *Lusitania* survivors were inclined to agree with Colonel House that war was inevitable. Seaman Mahoney was already back at sea, continuing his now-personal war against Germany. Bernard and Donald were both in the British

Army. Dr. Fisher and Dorothy Conner were busy with hospital and canteen work in France.

But some, like Theodate Pope and Alice Middleton, were unable to act. Still sick and stunned by the experience, they remained in their hospital beds.

D. A. Thomas, nothing daunted, was just beginning his own counterattack, as he conferred with Whitehall for a return trip to the United States. The purpose: to buy ammunition and other military supplies for Great Britain.

On May 24 America was reminded anew of its loss. The liner *New York* docked with some *Lusitania* survivors, and below decks, the silent company of the less fortunate. Charles Frohman was among them.

Next day thousands lined Fifth Avenue in front of Temple Emanu-El for Frohman's funeral. Inside, sorrowing multitudes, including actors, actresses, authors, and theater managers, heard Rabbi Joseph Silverman intone the burial prayers. The casket was adorned simply with a cluster of violets from Maude Adams.

Charles Plamondon and Mary had also come home on the *New York*. The family doctor reported that her dress was still soot-covered, and that Charles' watch had stopped at two-thirty. His diary was almost intact in his pocket. Chicago turned out in mourning for a solemn requiem mass at the Holy Name Cathedral. Police officer Lavin, holding back the crowd, wept unashamedly.

In England, Elizabeth Duckworth, after a period of recuperation, put on her sturdy gray cotton, bought a new lunch basket, and reported for duty at the Royal Arsenal ammunition factory in Blackstone.

As the war in Europe gained momentum, anti-German feeling rose to a feverish pitch. Herbert Ehrhardt found it

expedient to change his name to "Hereward," and Robert
Wiemann legally became "Barnes." It didn't matter that
they themselves had almost fallen victims to the Prussian
war machine.

On June 15 Lord Mersey, who had handled the *Titanic*
investigation, opened the inquiry "into the loss of the steamship *Lusitania*." During six sessions in Westminster Hall, he
and assessors of the Board of Trade heard the testimony of
thirty-six survivors, including Captain Turner, and other
"qualified" witnesses.

Published findings were substantially the same as those of
Coroner Horgan at Kinsale. Captain Turner and the steamship company were absolved of blame, the guilt placed,
"solely with those who plotted and with those who committed
the crime."

During the summer of 1915, members of the American Society for Psychical Research reported visitations from Edwin
Friend. They said his face appeared "flushed" as he denounced Germany's "dastardly deed." The society's journal
noted the appearance of Elbert Hubbard at one seance as a
witty "interloper."

On July 28 Rita Jolivet's sister, Inez Vernon, decided life
was too lonely without her husband, George, who had died
at the side of Frohman. Sitting before her dressing table in
her New York apartment, in evening dress enhanced by her
jewels, she shot herself through the head.

Wedding bells were ringing in Manchester, England, for
Gerta Nielson, a milliner, and John Welsh, engineer. They
were fellow *Lusitania* survivors. It had been a shipboard ro-
mance and, just as in the story books, he had kept her afloat
until rescued. Olive North became engaged to Percy Hanson,
a sailor from the *Juno*.

Robert Leith, the Marconi operator, and Les Morton, the young lookout, were presented to the Court of St. James.

As 1916 began, the Lordship of Rhondda of Llanwern was created for D. A. Thomas. The *Lusitania* survivor, in addition to his newly obtained seat in the House of Lords, was becoming one of Britain's most powerful wartime figures, with appointments as Food Controller and Minister of Health on the horizon. A busy and ubiquitous man, he would be speaking on pig breeding in Wales one day, opening National Baby Week in London the next.

One day before the first anniversary of the *Lusitania*'s sinking, Theodate Pope found herself sufficiently recovered to embark on a different sort of voyage. She was married, in Farmington, Connecticut, to former Ambassador to Russia, John Wallace Riddle.

Next day, May 7, Captain Turner was in New York harbor, in command of the freighter *Ultonia*, his cargo mostly mules. He was having crew trouble and had to call on the British consul to settle their wage disagreements.

The New York *Herald* published an anniversary edition, with black-bordered columns, as it had a few days after the torpedoing. Editorially it deplored the fact that Germany had not "atoned" for the act.

On June 1 the greatest naval battle the world had ever known thundered around Jutland Bank and ended the threat that had been posed by the Kaiser's Grand Fleet. Rear Admiral H. L. A. Hood, lost with his *Invincible*, was to take his place alongside of Nelson and Drake—the humiliation of Dover and Queenstown, his abortive attempts to aid the *Lusitania* erased forever.

After more than a year, legal reverberations from the *Lusitania* still continued throughout the land. Mrs. May Davies

Hopkins, for one, was awarded by the courts a 40,000-dollar life insurance settlement on a policy taken out by her late husband, A. L. Hopkins, president of the Newport News Shipbuilding and Drydock Company. Most beneficiaries were still fighting for such consolations—whether from insurance companies or from claims they were endeavoring to institute against the American government, the British government, the Cunard Company, and even Berlin.

On New Year's Day, 1917, Captain Turner took the transport *Ivernia* out of Marseilles, en route to Salonika. He had just set foot in Liverpool, after a narrow escape from a submarine, when he was rushed across France to relieve an ailing friend, Captain Arthur Rostron. Under strangely similar circumstances he had taken the place of Captain Paddy Dow before the *Lusitania*'s last sailing from Liverpool. Off Cape Matapan, Greece, the *Ivernia* was torpedoed with the loss of 153 soldiers and crewmen. Moments before the doomed liner plunged beneath the Mediterranean, Will Turner swam from his bridge, then clung to a chair while awaiting rescue.

Cunard decided its commodore had used up his luck. With two and a half years till retirement, he was made relief captain at Glasgow and Liverpool. Alfred A. Booth, grateful for the aging man's services, arranged for him to be decorated with the Order of the British Empire.

Walther Schwieger's luck held somewhat longer. He became Germany's sixth ranking submarine ace, sinking 190,-000 tons of enemy shipping before his *U-88* was lost off Denmark in September, 1917. He and his crew fell victim to the submarine's most dreaded menace, the decoy or Q-ship and her depth charges. It was believed the *U-88* also ran into a mine field in her attempt to escape.

The ship that was fatal to Schwieger was HMS *Stonecrop*.

Among those serving on another of His Majesty's ships in the same squadron was Robert J. Clarke; he had been a bellboy on the *Lusitania*.

In America, war clouds grew darker. On January 31, 1917, Germany announced her policy of unrestricted submarine warfare, which in effect had commenced as early as May 7, 1915. Less than a month later another Cunarder, the *Laconia*, went down in a snowstorm off the Old Head of Kinsale. Mrs. Mary Hoy and her daughter Elizabeth, of Chicago, froze to death in a lifeboat.

Incidents such as this hastened President Wilson's decision to arm American merchant vessels. As the number of sinkings mounted, the revelation of a note in which Germany allegedly tried to incite Mexico and Japan to war with the United States did little to soothe the nation.

On March 17 three medium-sized American freighters, the *City of Memphis, Vigilancia,* and *Illinois* were torpedoed in the war zone. A total of twenty-four Americans were lost.

Other ships followed the three to the bottom, other Americans perished.

Finally, on April 2, at 8:30 P.M., President Wilson went before a hushed Senate Chamber to ask that the existence of a state of war with Germany be declared. It was Monday, in Holy Week. By Good Friday the House of Representatives had completed the ratification. And at 1:13 P.M. that Friday Wilson signed the declaration, expressing his certainty that "America has found herself."

The *Lusitania*, in the sum total of all the dreary and tragic events leading to war, certainly had not been forgotten.

EPILOGUE

~~~~~~

Forty-one years is a long time, and New York doesn't look, smell, or even feel very much the way it did that spring morning of 1915 when newsreel photographers shot rolls of film at the foot of 13th Street.

Yet Pier 54, rotting and rat-infested, strewn with broken glass, plaster, and posters, still endures like a haunted house to whisper, "The *Lusitania* sailed from here."

Another war has since come and gone. The people of many nations rose in indignation once more as newspaper cartoonists and editorial writers lashed out in tones peculiarly reminiscent of their fathers'. The mounting storm seethed over the entire world before it finally died down, even as in 1918. Yet somehow, the name *Lusitania* and all it implies has become timeless. Every child reads it in first history books, even though there is little more than a mention. Young marine engineers study the great liner as lawyers do Blackstone.

Up until World War II attempts persisted to get down to the wreck, some eleven miles off the Old Head of Kinsale, and recover legendary millions in gold bullion from her waterbound strongrooms. In 1935 a British diver, Jim Jarrat, believed he actually walked across the plates of the sunken Cunarder, some 300 feet deep.

Though Jarrat believed the *Lusitania* rested on her port side, an underwater sound camera more recently checked her position as it traced her silhouette with startling clarity. It showed the mighty vessel apparently on even keel and headed in the general direction of St. George's Channel and Liverpool Bar, on a voyage interrupted by a torpedo. Irish fishermen, attesting to the same thing, report the shadows of her mast tips at low tide.

Throughout the world, wherever veteran divers and salvage men gather, they speculate on how one yet might descend to the world of watery darkness, immense pressure —and ghosts—to explore the hull of the *Lusitania* and perhaps even discover its reputed treasure. For it is one of the most famous and portentous sunken liners on the earth's ocean beds. Only a very few from World War II are any larger or caused a greater loss of life.

Perhaps forty survivors remember the *Lusitania,* and the events that transpired aboard it. Yet, almost to a person, they admit that the perspective of time has not enabled them to understand just what the catastrophe was all about—or what, if anything, the destruction of so many human beings meant in the greater web and perplexity of existence.

Many lived to find a peace that seemed unattainable in the waters off Ireland that May afternoon. Captain Turner still had eighteen years in which to enjoy his garden, his dog, cat, and pipe in Great Crosby. Elizabeth Duckworth remained vigorous for most of her years, finally sleeping away in 1955 at the age of ninety-two in Taftville, Connecticut; while Second Engineer Andrew Cockburn, eighty-four, died in Southampton, England, the same year.

In Farmington, Connecticut, the colonial mansion that she designed has not rung since 1946 to the sound of Theodate Pope Riddle's voice. Yet over the fireplace mantel, in her library, a hint endures of the part which the ocean, its ships and time itself played in her life: a sea painting by Whistler and an antique clock which ticktocks, ticktocks.

In South Paris, Maine, James Brooks, eighty-two, sits under a shade tree on his lawn and dreams of the future.

ACKNOWLEDGMENTS

~~~~~~

We wish to express our appreciation to these survivors of the *Lusitania* for their devoted assistance: William M. Adams, Virginia Bruce Loney Abbott, Robert Barnes (Wiemann), A. A. Bestic, James H. Brooks, the Reverend Robert J. Clarke, Archibald Douglas Donald, Dorothy Conner Dugger, Avis Dolphin Foley, Matthew Freeman, Elizabeth Hampshire Graham, Hugh Johnston, Beatrice Williams Harper, Olive North Hanson, Herbert W. Hereward (Ehrhardt), Parry Jones, J. I. Lewis, Mrs. Ethel M. L. Lines, Thomas Mahoney, Alice Middleton McDougall, Dr. R. J. R. Mecredy, Leslie N. Morton, Florence M. Padley, Irene E. Paynter, John Preston-Smith, Viscountess Margaret (Mackworth) Rhondda, Mrs. E. M. West.

We are particularly grateful for the graphic accounts left behind by certain survivors who are no longer living: Oliver P. Bernard, Charles E. Lauriat, Jr., Elizabeth Duckworth, Professor I. B. Stoughton Holbourn, Theodate Pope Riddle.

And we owe much to a rather vast assemblage of men and women who are relatives or friends of the passengers of the *Lusitania* or in some way have been able to shed additional

241

light on the events surrounding it: Mabel Avery (Captain Turner's housekeeper), Sheila Acton, Bruce Bernard, Florence Stackhouse Bailey, Thomas A. Bailey, George Ball, Frank Braynard, W. J. Cull, Charles Cowper, Ralph Cropley, Lorrie Dolphin, Herbert F. Goodrich, Mrs. I. B. Stoughton Holbourn, Elbert Hubbard II, William Harmar, G. Percy Harris, T. J. Healy, John J. Horgan, John A. Johnston, M. Constance Karney, S. Alex Leith, Patrick Little, George Loynd, Peter Mason, Mayne Murphy, Seumas O'Neill, Lily O'Connell, Carol Patton, Harvey E. Parry, Charles Ambrose Plamondon, James F. Reilly, the Reverend Charles E. Sheedy, C.S.C., William Smith, Gertrude O. Tubby, Robert Withington Tucker, N. H. Turner, Alfred Gwynne Vanderbilt, Jr., William H. Vanderbilt, E. M. Watson, Emma E. Yaggie.

. . . and also to many companies and organizations, including the Cunard Steamship Co., Ltd., Esso Petroleum Co., Ltd., Gibbs and Cox, Merritt Chapman and Scott Co., Moran Towing Co., N. Y., N. H. and Hartford RR., Newport News Shipbuilding and Drydock Co., Seaman's Church Institute, Stacey and Co., the Marconi Corp. (Richard Griffiths), the United States Lines, the U.S. Coast and Geodetic Survey, and the U.S. Department of State.

. . . to these newspapers for assisting us in a variety of helpful ways: Akron *Beacon Journal,* Boston *Globe,* Boston *Herald,* Boston *Transcript, Christian Science Monitor,* Chicago *Tribune,* Chicago *Daily News,* Cleveland *Plain Dealer,* Cleveland *Press,* East Aurora *Advertiser,* Kansas City *Star,* Los Angeles *Times,* New York *Times,* New York *Herald Tribune,* New York *Daily News,* New York *Sun,* New York *World and Telegram,* Norwich (Conn.) *Bulletin,* Pittsburgh *Post-Gazette,* Pittsburgh *Press,* San Francisco *Bulletin,* San Francisco *Chronicle,* St. Louis *Post-Dispatch,* Seattle *Post-In-*

ACKNOWLEDGMENTS

telligencer, Toronto *Star,* the North American Newspaper Alliance.

. . . and, overseas: *Daily Record* (Glasgow), *Daily Sketch* (London), *Daily Mirror* (London), *Daily News* (London) and (Manchester), *Evening Dispatch of Edinburgh, Evening Herald* (Dublin), *Irish Independent,* London *Times,* Manchester *Guardian, Sunday Pictorial* (London), Sydney *Herald, Weekly Scotsman,* Worcester *Daily Times*

. . . to these magazines: *American Historical Review, Current Opinion, Current History, Journal of the American Society of Psychical Research, Literary Digest, Living Age, London Illustrated News, Marine Engineering, Naval Architect, The Sphere, The Spectator, Scientific Monthly, Stage, American Mercury, Lippincott's.*

. . . to these libraries, museums, and their helpful librarians and curators: The New York Public Library, and the many there who gave assistance, especially Robert Hug; the Boston Public Library, the Chicago Public Library, Cleveland Public Library, Hillstead Museum (Farmington, Connecticut), especially Mrs. Frisbie, San Francisco Public Library, Stamford Public Library, Darien Public Library, Gloucester Public Library, Library of the British Information Services, Imperial War Museum (London), Submarine Library of the General Dynamics Corp., Smithsonian Institution, Museum of the City of New York, especially May Davenport Seymour, National Archives.

Also of mention is a lately received letter from Otto Rikowski, of Hamburg, Germany, who states he is probably the last surviving member of the crew of the *U-20* who was aboard when the submarine torpedoed the *Lusitania.*

BOOKS THAT HAVE
BEEN MOST VALUABLE
SOURCE MATERIAL

Allen, George Henry. *The Great War*. Philadelphia, G. Barrie's Sons, 1915-1921.

Bernard, Oliver P. *Cock Sparrow*. London, Jonathan Cape, 1936.

Bergen, Klaus. *U-Boat Stories*. London, Constable and Co., n.d.

Churchill, Winston. *World Crisis*. New York, Charles Scribner's Sons, 1923.

Corbett, Sir Julian S. *Naval Operations*. London, Longmans Green, 1920.

Ellis, Frederick D. *The Tragedy of the Lusitania*. Privately printed, 1915.

——*The Encyclopedia Americana*.

——*The Encyclopedia Britannica*.

Frost, Wesley. *German Submarine Warfare*. New York, D. Appleton & Co., 1918.

Gibson, R. H., and Maurice Prendergast. *The German Submarine War*. London, Constable and Co., 1931.

Hashagen, Ernst. *U-Boats Westward!* London, G. B. Putnam's Sons, 1931.

Hendricks, Burton J. *The Life and Letters of Walter Hines Page.* New York, Doubleday, Page & Co., 1922.

Horgan, John J. *Parnell to Pearse.* Dublin, Browne and Nolan, Ltd., 1948.

Horne, Charles, and Walter F. Austin (eds.). *Source Records of the Great War.* National Alumni Press, 1923.

Lauriat, Charles E. *The Lusitania's Last Voyage.* Boston, Houghton Mifflin and Co., 1915.

March, Francis A. *History of the World War.* United Publishers of the United States and Canada, 1919.

Marcosson, Isaac F., and Daniel Frohman. *Charles Frohman, Manager and Man.* New York, Harper & Brothers, 1916.

Seymour, Charles (ed.). *Intimate Papers of Colonel House.* Boston, Houghton Mifflin and Co., 1926.

Shay, Felix. *Elbert Hubbard of East Aurora.* New York, William H. Wise and Co., 1926.

Ward, Maisie. *Father Maturin.* London, Longmans Green, 1920.

INDEX

Adams, Maude, 77, 194, 231
Aleppo, Cunard steamer, 66
Alexander, Mrs. Charles B., 28
Allan, Lady Marguerite, and twin daughters Anna and Gwen, passengers, 194-195, 210
Allen, Dorothy, First Class passenger, 71, 220
American Society for Psychical Research, 232
Anderson, engineer, 67
Anderson, J. C., Staff Captain, 62, 125, 133, 211, 217
Antisubmarine precautions aboard *Lusitania,* 60, 87
Aquitania, Cunard liner, 37, 38, 67
Arcona, German ship, 51
Askin, Harry, 187-188

Barnes, Robert. *See* Wiemann, Robert
Barrymore, Ethel, 37, 77
Bates, Lindon W., passenger, 148-149
Belasco, David, 30
Belgian relief, tour of Mme de Page on behalf of, 28
Benedict XV, Pope, 225
Bennington, steam trawler, sunk by U-boat, 55
Bergensfjord, liner, 57
Bernard, Oliver P., First Class passenger, 101-102, 217-218, 230; after torpedoing, 139-142, 158-161; after leaving ship, 168, 185, 207-208; quoted, on temporary morgues for victims of disaster, 217-218
Bernstorff, Count Johann von, German Ambassador to United States, 34
Bestic, Albert A., Junior Third Officer, 99; after torpedoing, 117, 205-206

Bilbrough, George, Second Class passenger, 75, 217; after leaving ship, 173
Bilicke, Mr. and Mrs. A. C., passengers, 116, 221
Bird, May, stewardess on *Lusitania,* 138
Blackout aboard *Lusitania,* 60, 87
Bluebell, fishing boat, to rescue of *Lusitania* passengers, 122, 204-206, 219
Booth, Alfred A., Chairman of Cunard Board, 26, 234
Borkum Reef Lightship, 51
Boston *Globe,* 195
Bowen, Edward B., 31-32, 191
Boy-Ed, Captain, of German Embassy, 77
Brisbane, Arthur, 192
Bristol, British battleship, 56
British Admiralty, submarine warnings by, 14, 64-65, 86-89, 92, 93
Brock, mine sweeper, to rescue of *Lusitania* passengers, 213
Brooks, James H., passenger, 45-46, 61, 92, 102, 216, 239; after torpedoing, 108, 132-133, 147; after leaving ship, 167, 181-182, 207
Brooks, Mrs. James H., 45-46
Brown, John, 62
Brown, Mrs. William H., 192
Bryan, William Jennings, 230
Bryce, Archibald, Chief Engineer, 26, 62-64, 67-68, 84, 107

Cameronia, Cunard liner, 34, 57
Campbell, Alexander, passenger, 35, 210
Canada, reaction to news of disaster, 194-195
Candidate, Harrison liner, torpedoed by U-boat, 84

247